Fundamental Principles of Marxism: political economy & philosophy

Fundamental Principles of Marxism:
political economy & philosophy

Daniel Rubin

NEW YORK
INTERNATIONAL PUBLISHERS

Acknowledgements

"Marxism," "collectivity" and "individual responsibility" are closely interdependent concepts. That is why in writing this book I sought and received the help of a number of leading U.S. Marxists.

Dee Myles, Libero Della Piana, Betty Smith, Adam Tenney and Sam Webb read and discussed my initial draft overall. I made revisions and we then discussed the manuscript chapter by chapter in two sessions. Many useful changes resulted. Marilyn Bechtel then edited the manuscript, making helpful suggestions and improving its readability. Betty Smith also helped with the editing and carried out the printing and publishing process at International Publishers.

I thank all these co-workers for their many contributions. But in the end I take responsibility for everything that is in, or not in, the book. There is nothing in the book with which I disagree and nothing has been left out of the book that I would have wanted in it. I have no doubt that use of the book for discussion groups, classes, schools, and individual use, as well as new developments every few years, will reveal the need for changes in the text.

Contents

Preface to Second Edition

The Preface to the 1st edition was completed before it became clear that Barack Obama might win the Democratic Party nomination and then be elected President. It was also written before the full onset of the most profound economic crisis since the Great Depression. As a result, there is barely initial analysis of these two critical events: the economic crisis is discussed in Chapter 2 in the sections that deal with the economic cycle, and on financialization. The 2008 Elections are discussed in Chapter 5.

In this 2nd Edition, I have chosen not to attempt to update these subjects, as there are ever new developments in both the Obama administration and the movements around it, and in the economy, while the fundamentals already discussed in the text remain relevant. Other books and articles on these subjects will be needed for a full Marxist treatment as they continue to develop.

One point, however, needs mention. The ultra-right no longer dominates the political landscape, including the Executive and Legislative branches of the Federal Government. They suffered a major defeat with the election of Barack Obama and the new Congress. We are now in an uneven, irregular transition to complete the defeat of the ultra-right political tendency and the sector of monopoly capital that dominates it, and move forward to the strategic stage of radically curbing the power of the monopoly capitalists as a whole. So far, just a few initial blows are being aimed at monopoly as a whole.

Daniel Rubin, New York City
December 2009

Preface

The pundits of capitalism would have us believe Marxism and socialism are dead, proven a failure by the collapse of the Soviet Union and the socialist countries of Eastern Europe, and the alleged return to capitalism of China and Vietnam. According to them, Marxism has been proven wrong both by events and theoretically. But looking around the world, the infuences of Marxism and socialism are growing in Latin America, Asia, and the other continents. This book seeks to show why the infuence of Marxism is growing again and what value it has for the working people of our country in their struggle for a better life.

In examining the main aspects of Marxism and how they can be of great aid to the struggle for progress, we do not start empty-handed. Many useful books exist. This book, however, seeks to cover all major aspects of Marxism in one short volume and also update it, while building on its fundamentals and applying its methodology to new developments.

The last book widely available in English that attempted to present the fundamentals of Marxism from the standpoint of its orthodox advocates, associated with the Communist Party USA, was "Introduction to Marxism" (1951) by the British Marxist Emile Burns. A slightly revised edition by International Publishers (IP) in the 1970s has been out of print for some years. To find an exposition of the fundamentals of Marxism, either introductory or more complete but not yet advanced, written by a U.S. author and based on U.S. experience, one must search the early years when socialists and communists were becoming differentiated after the Communist Party was founded in September 1919.

In 1960 a 600-page Soviet text, "The Fundamentals of Marxism-Leninism," appeared in a limited English edition. Each chapter was prepared by a committee of academicians from the Academy of Sciences under the overall editorship of Otto Kuusinen. Kuusinen, a co-worker of Lenin, a Secretary of the Communist International at the time of the Second Congress and long a member of the Political

Bureau of the Communist Party of the Soviet Union, returned to his native Finland in the mid-1960s to serve as Chairman of the Communist Party of Finland. That text served two purposes. It is the only text in English covering all major subjects of Marxism-Leninism in some detail. It attempts to free Marxism-Leninism from most of the theoretical and practical mistakes introduced under the influence of the cult of Joseph Stalin. It accomplishes this primarily by refuting a "well known thesis" and then quoting Stalin, usually without identifying him by name as the author.

Useful volumes in English presenting summaries of major subjects of Marxism include John Eaton, "Political Economy" (IP 1950, revised 1966); Maurice Cornforth, "Dialectical Materialism" (IP 1953, revised 1968) and "Historical Materialism" (IP 1954, revised 1968)—all by British Marxists; and French Marxist Georges Politzer's "Elementary Principles of Philosophy," written in the late 1930s and published by IP in 1976.

Valuable texts on such subjects by Soviet scholars, published in English, include V.G. Afanasayev, "Dialectical Materialism" and "Historical Materialism" (IP 1987); L. Leontyev, "Political Economy: A Condensed Course" (IP 1975); and P.I. Nikitin, "Fundamentals of Political Economy," (Progress Publishers 1983) as well as many earlier works.

U.S. authors have also presented aspects of these major subjects of Marxism. These volumes include Howard Selsam, "What is Philosophy?" (IP 1938), and Selsam and Harry Martel, "Reader in Marxist Philosophy" (IP 1978). Works on economics include Hyman Lumer, "Is Full Employment Possible?" (New Century Publishers 1962) and "Poverty: Its Roots and Future" (IP 1965); Victor Perlo, "Empire of High Finance" (IP 1957) and "Super Profits & Crises: Modern U.S. Capitalism" (IP 1988).

Henry Winston wrote "Strategy for a Black Agenda" (IP 1973) and "Class, Race and Black Liberation" (IP 1977), concerning national oppression of the African American people and its connection with the class struggle. There are also collections of writings by Gus Hall on the working class, class struggle and racism: "Working Class USA" (IP 1987) and "Fighting Racism" (IP 1985), and by James Jackson on socialism and national oppression of African Americans. Jackson's "Revolutionary Tracings in World Politics and Black

Liberation" (IP 1974) contains important documents on the theory of the "Negro question" from the 1950s, and his "The Bold Bad '60s" (IP 1992) is reportage of the Martin Luther King decade of struggles. Two editions of Victor Perlo's "Economics of Racism" (IP 1975, 1996) apply Marxist analysis to this important subject.

Lenin, of course, wrote his own popular summary of Marxism in his essay, "Karl Marx" (Collected Works, Vol. 21, p. 43, 1914). And Marx and Engels wrote the most famous summary of Marxism in "The Communist Manifesto" (1848, IP ed. 1948). IP published a very useful collection of introductory works, "Introduction to Marx, Engels, Marxism," in 1987. I edited a collection of excerpts from the classics, organized within 17 topics much as an introduction to Marxism would be organized, which was published by the Chelsea Fund for Education, Inc., in 2004 under the title, "Marx, Engels, Lenin, For a Better World: Excerpts from the Classics."

The pages that follow attempt a systematic presentation and discussion of the major subjects of Marxism, based on U.S. experience.

Here is an introduction to Marxism for those who first become interested in the subject. It answers the question, What is Marxism? and how and why it came into being. It makes an argument for Marxism's validity, usefulness and importance. But it is not simply an essay, arguing for the validity and usefulness of Marxism; it also presents the subject matter of Marxism systematically and relatively extensively—though it is not an exhaustive textbook covering all aspects of Marxism.

For those who already consider themselves Marxists, it brings together the major subjects of Marxism in a coherent, interdependent way, makes major applications specifically to the U.S., and using Marxist tools, updates major aspects of Marxist theory—for example, the current transnational monopoly phase of the monopoly capitalist, imperialist stage. It updates Marxism in many fields, taking into account both the achievements of the world Communist movement in the Soviet Union, Cuba, China, etc. and the failures and inadequacies in both theory and practice in the Stalin years and in the collapse of socialism in the Soviet Union and Eastern Europe. This "updating" takes place within the consensus of the world Communist movement and especially that of the Communist Party USA, though the author is responsible for all particular judgments.

9

In this book the sequence of subjects is changed from the earlier Burns and Soviet models. Usually a book on the fundamentals of Marxism begins with the most general and then moves on to the most particular. Such a book begins with the most universal of objective processes—dialectical materialism, then historical materialism, then the political economy of capitalism. Then it moves to the subjective side: who the forces for progress are, their strategy and tactics to move in a progressive direction, toward socialism. Finally, socialism and the organizations necessary to win it—the trade unions, the Communist Party and the Young Communist League—are discussed.

Instead, this book begins where most people begin who are considering Marxism and socialism, either casually or seriously. It begins with the big social problems that are seriously bothering large numbers of people. First it defines those problems, then it poses the big questions that naturally arise. Are these problems inherent in capitalism? Can they be eliminated from capitalism, or ameliorated, while capitalism still exists? If they cannot be eliminated, does that condemn capitalism to the scrap-heap of history? If so, then what follows? Socialism or something else? Can socialism create the conditions for the elimination of those social problems? If socialism is the answer, how can it be won? Who needs to do what to win socialism?

The second chapter and the rest of the book follow a logical sequence in providing Marxist answers to the questions posed in the introductory chapter. Chapters 2 and 3 deepen the answers as to why capitalism causes, and benefits from, the major social problems of the people. In Chapter 2, **The Political Economy of Capitalism**, proof is given that capitalism is a system based on exploitation of the working class by the capitalist class, based on the drive for maximum profits. The connection of exploitation and maximum profits with the big social problems is discussed.

In Chapter 3, **Historical Materialism**, we continue to show why capitalism gives birth to or aggravates existing major social problems. We discuss the interrelationships of all the major aspects of the capitalist socioeconomic formation, and how and why it developed out of prior social formations. We show the decisive role of the economy, and how it relates to all the other major aspects of society, particularly the political structure. We discuss how it is possible to have laws of social development—even when we are dealing with millions of peo-

10

ple with their own capacity to think and act. We learn that the "necessity" contained in such laws appears only through the accidents of human activity.

Chapter 4, **Socialism**, discusses the theory of why socialism follows capitalism, as expressed in the Marxist classics. Lenin's contributions to the theory and practice of socialism are explained. Next we examine how U.S. history, culture and existing conditions will shape its socialism in many new ways while still expressing the basic character of socialism. Then we look at socialism as it is currently developing in different areas of the world: China, Vietnam, Cuba, Venezuela and Latin America generally. Finally, we look back at socialism in the USSR under Stalin's leadership and from then until its collapse in 1992, to learn from these experiences for the future.

In the next three chapters, we discuss how to go from where we are now all the way to socialism. The first part of Chapter 5, **The Theory of Socialist Revolution**, discusses strategy and tactics, the necessary social forces, and their role in winning socialism. Strategy and tactics, and their interrelationship, are clarifed, as are the various stages of struggle to reach the socialist goal. Here the role of the core social forces for social change are emphasized, beginning with the working class, and including the racially and nationally oppressed, the women and the youth.

In Chapter 6, **Marxist Methodology: Tool of Struggle**, is elaborated. How do Marxists reach their conclusions when examining objective developments, in deciding their strategic and tactical policies and their everyday organizational activity? We explain the decisive role of a working-class outlook on all questions, along with the application of the main laws of dialectics and some secondary laws of how change and development take place.

Finally, in Chapter 7, **Organizations Necessary for Winning Progress and Socialism**, there is discussion of why trade unions, the Communist Party and the Young Communist League are necessary for the struggle for progress and socialism and the role of each. The role of other democratic organizations representing additional sectors of the population and social issues is also discussed.

A glossary of 71 Marxist concepts concludes the book. Each concept is briefly explained. We hope that you find these innovations helpful in gaining a fuller, better grasp of Marxist thought and methodology, and in deciding whether for you it is an indispensable tool for living, working and struggling for a better world.

Daniel Rubin
New York City, January 2009

Fundamental Principles of Marxism: political economy & philosophy

1 The Great Social Ills of Our Time: How Marx, Engels and Lenin Took Them On

Introduction

Our discussion of the fundamentals of Marxism begins with a listing and examination of the biggest social problems of our times. Is their existence due to capitalism? Can they be partially or completely eliminated while capitalism exists? What will follow capitalism—socialism, or something else? Can socialism make it possible to eliminate all the great social ills?

Next we discuss in broad outline the role of Marx, Engels and Lenin in answering these questions, both in theory and through practical activity. The main challenges to Marxism are outlined. That is followed by a discussion of the major social ills, in terms of why the current existence of each serves the needs of the capitalist system and its dominant capitalist class.

Defining and describing the great social ills

The "War to Defeat Fascism and End All Wars" (World War II) has been followed by one war after another, the deaths of millions and wounding of many millions more. Millions have been driven from their homes and trillions of dollars and resources have been wasted and destroyed in the process. The danger of nuclear war that could wipe out all life on the planet hangs over our heads.

Threats to the environment have already caused irreparable harm. All life on the planet is seriously threatened. The world economy, and especially that of the major capitalist powers, is developing in an unsustainable way.

Democratic rights are seriously eroded in our country and in much of the world. Tens of millions in the U.S. and billions worldwide are deprived of democratic rights and suffer national, racial and gender oppression, which undermine the conditions of life of all working people and erode their unity in struggle. Elections here and in much of the world show that democratic processes are seriously limited.

The working class in the U.S. and around the world is increasingly exploited and finds it harder to make ends meet. Its income is stagnant or declining both in absolute terms and relative to the rising income and wealth of the top capitalists. In our country, 36 million live below the poverty line and 28 million depend on food stamps to survive, while a handful of multi-billionaires get richer by the second. (The current economic crisis will be discussed in Chapter 3.)

Pandemics like HIV-AIDS, malaria and tuberculosis take the lives of millions while prevention and treatment are greatly limited for lack of funds. Tens of millions in our country, and billions worldwide, suffer hunger, poverty and unemployment while experiencing inadequate housing, health care and education.

The needs of youth are not met for education, recreation, culture, job preparation, and a progressive, democratic outlook on life. Instead, they are used as cannon fodder, and written off as an unneeded generation, condemned to a life without hope or confidence in a bright future.

Working people are denied a cultural life affirming the finest values to which the working class and humanity aspire—peace, equality, justice and democracy. Many cultural activities are constantly on the brink of financial collapse, most cultural workers are poorly paid and most live performances are too expensive for working people.

Is it really accidental that society's great problems exist and even grow under capitalism's dominance, or is there a causal relationship between capitalism and their existence? Spokespersons for capitalism have repeatedly claimed capitalism can eliminate them worldwide, but the best that can be said is that they have been eased temporarily here or there, mainly as a result of popular struggles.

The big questions

If the major social ills are inherent in capitalism, impossible of complete, lasting elimination and in many cases getting steadily worse, what does that say about the future of capitalism and about the likelihood that it will continue to exist? Can socialism be a desirable and logical replacement? Is any other replacement possible? If socialism is the answer, in our country and worldwide, how can that come about?

The great social scientists, political thinkers, leaders and activists Karl Marx (1818-1883), Frederick Engels (1820-1895) and Vladimir Lenin (1870-1924) founded the outlook, movement and organizations known as Marxism or Marxism-Leninism. They sought answers to these and similar questions.

What Marx, Engels and Lenin did

Building on the ideas of German philosophers such as Georg W.F. Hegel and Ludwig Feuerbach, British political economists like David Ricardo and French socialists like Charles Fourier and Henri de Saint Simon, Marx and Engels answered in broad outline the connection between capitalism and the universal social problems.

They explained the basic nature of capitalism and the main laws of its development that gave rise to the major problems of society during its existence. These laws that Marx and Engels discovered continue to be expressed, but in ever new ways and under ever new specific conditions. When capitalism underwent a major change from the "free competitive" capitalism that Marx and Engels knew to monopoly capitalism—its imperialist stage—Lenin updated the laws of capitalism to analyze this great change and its social and political consequences. Since Lenin advanced the conclusions of Marxism in virtually all areas of life in the new stage of capitalism, the monopoly capitalist or imperialist stage, many add "Leninism" to "Marxism" to describe this ideology, this system of ideas. Marx, Engels and Lenin all objected to naming the ideology of the working class, which they had founded and developed, after themselves. In the U.S., given our cultural traditions, it seems ritualistic to always add "Leninism" to "Marxism."

Also drawing on Charles Darwin, Marx and Engels concluded that society as well as nature develops according to inherent laws in which necessity expresses itself only through chance occurrences and through human activity. Here, "chance" means that necessity may be expressed in many possible forms and at many possible times, reflecting the way events have unfolded and the balance of class and social forces that has evolved.

It is a law of capitalism that the working class will struggle against the capitalist class so long as capitalism exists. But we cannot tell from the existence of this law, or necessity, what forms and intensity of class struggle will take place when, where and with what outcome. Each episode of a strike, slowdown or workers' demonstration expresses that necessity, but the specific events through which the necessity is expressed are chance. These events have particular immediate causes and in that sense they are not accidents but are the results of those causes and have a high probability of accurate prediction. But their form, timing and outcome cannot be predicted just because the law exists. It is only possible to predict that the necessity will be expressed through one or another form of class struggle over a period of time.

Since these laws express themselves only in broad outline, and the timing of their assertion is not predictable, they not only allow for surprise and anomaly in the way they are expressed, but presume this will happen. Many of the laws Marx found in the development of the capitalist economy were "the law of the tendency" for something to happen. These were often partially countered by "laws of the tendency" of other, conflicting developments. Thus it is not possible to predict which tendency will predominate, especially in the short run.

But the laws of social development show that sooner or later capitalism, like its predecessors ancient slave society and feudalism, will need to be replaced and will be replaced by a new socioeconomic formation, communism, called "socialism" in its first phase, which will provide the opportunity to put a lasting end to the major social problems of capitalism.

Marx, Engels and Lenin also concluded that capitalism contained the seeds of its own demise. It gave rise to class and democratic struggle for the needs and interests of the working class and all other democratic sectors of the population that are exploited and oppressed as a result of capitalism's nature. These include the nationally and racially oppressed, the women and the youth. They found theoretically, and experienced practically, that only the working class would be capable of, and would find it necessary to lead the struggle for those needs and to replace capitalism with socialism.

Lenin, and most scholars after, analyzed Marxism and concluded it had three aspects, the first of these being its philosophy. The founders of Marxism advanced a philosophy that revealed there were universal laws of development, and the concept that existence is prior to thought; therefore, there is an objective existence independent of our mental conceptions. Truthful knowledge can be gained through practice, including various methods of scientific observation. They studied and elucidated the major laws of social development, from which they reached their conclusion that capitalism would be replaced by socialism. This part of Marxism, its philosophy, is called dialectical and historical materialism. It contains laws that assert if A is present, then B will follow, but always in a different particular form in various periods. If there is capitalism, there must be exploitation and class struggle, is such a law. Marxism also consists of theories such as the theory of surplus value (see Chapter 2), the existence of which are well proven but the operation of which can be modified in special cases.

The political economy of capitalism is also one of the essential components of Marxism. Political economy studies the production relations between people. It describes and proves the laws of capitalism's existence and development. In it Marx proves that the capitalist system compels the capitalists to pursue maximum profits, which they can accomplish only through constantly increasing the exploitation of the working class. Such profit-seeking, it turns out, is one of the main causes of the biggest social problems present during capitalism. We have experienced lately how "profit-seeking" impacts from production, to finance, credit and commerce generally, with extremely negative social results.

The philosophy and political economy of Marxism, based on laws of development of objective reality, are scientific in nature. The third part of Marxism is the theory of socialist revolution. This deals with the subjective side of things, what people need to do to move forward toward the winning of socialism and its actual establishment. It contains theories, principles and general conclusions from experience in struggle. It bases itself on the application of the first two aspects of Marxism—dialectical and historical materialism, and political economy.

The theory of socialist revolution deals with the theory and application of strategy and tactics to guide the struggle for progress and for socialism. It also contains Lenin's theory of the "party of the new type," and includes other organizations necessary to advance and win the struggle all the way to socialism, as well as how to apply these theories to the concrete situations and problems that arise.

Taken together, these three aspects of Marxism constitute a consistent, interdependent system of ideas—an ideology corresponding to the vital interests of the working class. Each class has one or more ideologies that express its particular outlook. As the ideology consistently corresponding to working class interests, Marxism needs to grow and develop, taking into account new developments and new expressions of existing necessities and learning from its mistakes and misperceptions. In doing so, it carries what remains valid and useful from the old into the new. It is not a rigid, dogmatic, unchanging view of reality. More than once Engels characterized Marxism as "a guide to action," not an instruction or prescription of what to do. And Lenin argued that the only "absolute" is change.

The attacks on Marxism

Ever since Marxist analysis was publicly introduced in "The Communist Manifesto," written by Marx and Engels in 1848, countless attempts have been made to refute Marxism on both a theoretical and a practical level. On the practical level, every victory of capitalism, any defeat of the working class and other forces for social progress, every weakness or failure of existing socialism, has been alleged to refute Marxism. The defeat of the Paris Commune in 1872 "proved" that Marxism was wrong. The collapse of socialism in the USSR and other Eastern European countries was declared the end of Marxism and socialism.

When Lenin began the New Economic Policy (NEP) in 1921, combining controlled state capitalism with direct socialist measures under working-class rule and Communist Party leadership, the capitalist media declared it proved the superiority of capitalism and said it would lead to restoration of full capitalism. In recent years the same is said of China: reintroduction of capitalist enterprise, even under working-class state control and Communist Party leadership, is cited as showing the failure of the socialist path and foretelling a return to capitalism.

Many attempts have been made to reject Marxism on a theoretical basis.

"Marxism and socialism are 'good ideas' but people are too selfish for them ever to be a practical success."

"The Marxism of Marx and Engels had some good ideas, but Lenin and Stalin produced a socialism in backward Russia that was of necessity authoritarian and anti-democratic."

"Marxism is economic determinism, while many more causes of development are at work."

"It is impossible to have laws of social development because millions of people are acting in many conflicting directions, according to their own 'free will.'"

"The Marxist concept of class and class struggle and of the role of the working class is invalid. Class is determined by a combination of factors, such as income, wealth, social status and self-conception. If we look at how people act, there is no consistent pattern based on class status."

"Dialectical materialism has no meaning. It is simply mysticism, especially the proposition of the 'negation of the negation.'"

"Marxism may have some significance in helping to understand the past, but it is not possible to predict the future, and Marxism cannot and does not make any contribution to that."

We shall discuss many of these propositions. Despite defeats, failures, mistakes and frequent burials, despite the many efforts of ruling classes around the world to destroy its influence, Marxism is on the upswing again and is the main outlook of hundreds of millions of people inside and outside Marxist parties. Next to the Bible, "The Communist Manifesto" is the world's most widely-read book. There is no region of the world, and scarcely a country, where there is not at least one party basing itself on Marxism and having considerable stature and influence on how events develop. In Latin America the influence of Marxism is growing rapidly among the many forces struggling for complete independence and an end to domination by the land-based oligarchy and big capital. Marxism is also a big influence in the new radical movements among indigenous people, landless peasants, workers, patriotic sections of the military, etc. Many are attracted by the real experiences of Cuba and Venezuela. New movements and organizations moving leftward are studying Marxism and creating new socialist and Marxist parties. All sections of working people around the world are influenced to one degree or another by the ideas of Marxism.

As Lenin said, "The Marxist doctrine is omnipotent because it is true." ("Three Sources and Three Component Parts of Marxism," 1913, CW Vol. 19, p. 23.) It cannot be eliminated from the world scene because it provides a way to gain authentic knowledge of the world in which we live and is a guide to how to change it for the better, even though it does not guarantee us against temporary errors in understanding that world.

It is the purpose of this book to show the reader why these characterizations of Marxism are both true and useful.

Marxism cannot be killed because there can be no capitalism without a working class. And capitalism's system of exploiting the working class gives rise to a class struggle by the working class to improve its living standards, and to end the horrible scourges of capitalism. The working class requires Marxism to accomplish these goals. Therefore, Marxism can suffer defeats, but it cannot be destroyed any more than the working class can be destroyed.

The causes of the social ills

In discussing the great social ills of today and their connection with capitalism, we recognize that a number of them first came into existence some time before capitalism. But with each new socioeconomic system, the forms of oppression, the particular aims of class domination, etc. change according to the needs of the new social system

Wars

Prior to ancient slave society, armed conflicts took place over such natural resources as land, water and food. More substantial wars began during ancient slave society and continued throughout feudalism and capitalism up to the present. Lenin agreed with Clausewitz that war was a continuation of political policy by other, military means.

As society advanced in organization, "war" was the instrument of the dominant class. In ancient slave society, the effort to expand the most important property holding, that of slaves, led to wars of conquest against neighbors to increase possession of land, food and water that in turn, required the labor of slaves. During feudalism, the struggle was over the most important property of the time, land-holdings with serfs attached. Under capitalism, the aim of war was to increase capitalist profit according to its different forms and the methods of obtaining it that developed in the different stages of capitalism—merchant capitalism, "free competitive" capitalism and monopoly capitalism (the imperialist stage).

The event that could set off a war might be quite removed from the basic economic causes. The assassination of Archduke Ferdinand in Sarajevo set off World War I. The actions of the leaders of different powers, long-standing national hatreds and competition and much more went into setting off the particular developments of World War I (1914-1918). But underlying them all was the growing economic domination of different areas of the world by Germany, Austria-Hungary and the other Central Powers, particularly Southeastern Europe, Africa, the Middle East and parts of South America. This domination grew through the export of capital to these places as well as control of the export of manufactured goods in exchange for raw materials. Such domination challenged the prior division of the world in relation to military occupation and political control. The other imperialist powers associated with the Entente—Britain, France, the U.S. and others—sought to strengthen their dominant position. Thus Lenin concluded that World War I was an unjust war on both sides. At base, war was still fought for the underlying class economic interests of the ruling class.

The particular aims of war have changed. The means of war and its effects have changed dramatically. Now we have war to conquer a country, to control its oil, to threaten a region that is oil-rich, to try to change its way of life, to tell the world the U.S. is militarily dominant and it is not afraid to use military force to achieve its aims. Now conventional arms can kill millions of soldiers and civilians in a matter of minutes, and can be used to occupy a country in hours. Weapons of mass destruction can kill millions in seconds, and can even threaten humanity and the existence of the planet. But so long as there is humanity and there is social development, these things cannot end resistance to occupation and oppression. Therefore, the proposition of Lenin that so long as capitalism existed in its monopoly capitalist, imperialist stage there would be motives for war, and while world wars and particular wars could be prevented or stopped, the inherent drive to war would still exist.

Environment

We have mainly become aware of the threats to the environment in the last 100 years; mass awareness is a product of less than 50 years. But in earlier socioeconomic systems, depletion of nature was acknowledged in relation to the need to move to areas with water and fertile soil, and where animals useful for food, clothing or shelter could be maintained. Again the prevailing economic system was an important factor in how human activity affected the uses of natural resources.

Now we are aware that human activity, whether unmindful or due to the pursuit of private profit, endangers every aspect of the environment. The connection of this extreme danger to the pursuit of maximum private profit is evident. Hiding behind claims that all problems can be cured without any loss of profits and without public expenditure cannot hide the main source of the immense, growing threat.

The fact that the first wave of socialist countries often denied the problem or engaged in wishful thinking about their ability to avoid it does not obscure the fact that pursuit of maximum profits by big capital is still the foremost problem. China, in a relatively early stage of building socialism, has only recently become conscious that significant measures to protect the environment are vital to the wellbeing of the masses of the people. The present unsustainable patterns of economic development which are leading to catastrophe are most evident and advanced in the developed capitalist world, but they are also present in all parts of the world.

Exploitation of the working class

As we will see, the basic source of the profits of the capitalist class is the exploitation of the working class, its unpaid labor. If we look at the working class of our country or of the world, the rate of exploitation continually grows, and the mass of surplus value and resulting profit grows. The working class produces more and receives back relatively less of what it produces. The drive to obtain maximum profits is built into capitalism and the only way the capitalist class as a whole can realize more profits is by increasing exploitation of the working class.

Democratic rights

The concept of what constitutes democratic rights, and what democratic rights working people require for a decent life, is changing. The social character of existence has grown tremendously, as Marx predicted it would. Now any important development anywhere in the world affects all working people, in our country and worldwide. How much more true that is with respect to events in our own country. Thus it is of ever-growing importance that we as individuals, and as members of the working class or of the middle strata, of different races and nationalities and genders, have an effective say in determining the multitude of decisions of governmental and legislative bodies at all levels. Such a democratic participation has become a growing necessity. Economic democracy, participating in making the basic decisions about the economy and about the enterprises we work in, has also become a prime necessity.

Such democracy is inimical to the very nature of capitalism. A strong tendency in the opposite direction is built into capitalism at this stage of its development. Of course, the absence of any democratic rights for the serfs and slaves of earlier societies is well known, but the status of "democratic rights" in present-day capitalism is growing worse. Lenin warned that monopoly capitalism and especially its finance capital aspect would give rise to increasing reactionary, anti-democratic tendencies within capitalist society. Soon after, capitalism, in its post-World War I political and economic crises, gave rise to fascism.

Now we are seeing that capitalism, even in its "bourgeois democratic" form of state rule, tends toward an increasingly authoritarian, anti-democratic rule. Among dangerous developments are the dominance of money and dirty tricks in elections, the stealing of elections, the suppression of the vote of African Americans and other nationally oppressed peoples, the corruption of Congress and the administration, in the interests of big capital. Also increased are all kinds of spying and curtailing of the right to speak, assemble and demonstrate; the undermining of labor's right to organize and strike; the destruction by executive and judicial decision of equality and affirmative action for

African Americans and other nationally oppressed, immigrants, and women.

The emergence of the prison-industrial complex, with 2 million predominantly nationally-oppressed semi-slave laborers is a major anti-democratic development, as is the use of torture against military prisoners. A mass extreme-right current is growing in U.S. life, nurtured by a section of transnational monopoly. While numerous theories and justifications are given for the anti-democratic trend in U.S. life, at bottom it strengthens big money's hold on government, and the use of government to maximize the profits of a particular section of big capital.

National and racial oppression

Oppression of one tribe, people, national group, or nationality by another, including wars, has been common from one social system to another, and each was connected with the property interests of the dominant class. But the rise of capitalism was connected with the rise of the nation-state and wars of conquest, in which nations, nationalities and peoples were made to be a part of the nation-state of another people, which then oppressed them. The capitalist class gained by the disunity of the workers of the different nations, and selected forms of oppression that produced more profit from the labor of the oppressed people for the same work. As is known, capitalist profits from slavery in the U.S. were the surplus profit that made rapid industrialization possible, and led to the U.S. capitalists becoming top dog internationally following World War I.

U.S. capitalists still realize billions of surplus profits from the unequal pay received by African Americans for the same work and work of comparable worth. They acquire additional billions as a result of lack of sufficient unity of workers across national and racial lines, as reflected in the continuing North-South differential in the U.S. Every aspect of U.S. life continues to reflect racism in some way. In elections, reaction consciously seeks to disfranchise African Americans, Latinos and Native Americans. Racism is involved in virtually every struggle whether it be on affordable housing, education, health care or other issues. Similar forms of special oppression impact Latinos, Native Americans, Asian and Pacific Islanders, Arab and other Middle Eastern peoples and immigrants to varying degrees. Super profits are made from all the inferior conditions of the nationally oppressed, and extra profits are reaped from white working people when insufficient unity weakens joint struggle against the capitalists. Much affirmative action for racially and nationally oppressed people, as for women, has been reversed by administrative or judicial decision.

While some African Americans and other oppressed peoples are somewhat better off economically, most have actually experienced a continuing decline, as they make up a large part of the lower half of Americans who have lost significant ground in income during recent years. Nor can we reduce the problem to "lingering ignorance and prejudice by white working people." The struggle for electoral power and in all other major battlefields, in which racism plays a big negative role, is at base a struggle to maximize profit for the few. The extreme political right thrives on racist threats and violence, such as the lynch rope symbol of slavery. Growing police brutality and use of unconstitutional methods is also a policy of the big bourgeoisie. (See Chapter 5 for a discussion of the election of Barack Obama as president.)

Oppression of women

Parallels exist in the special oppression of women, with the capitalist class extracting super profits from the disparity in pay for the same or comparable work. When workers are not united in economic struggles against the capitalists, men also suffer economically from women's oppression. Single mothers are among the poorest of all sections of the population.

Women's reproductive rights are under serious attack and the crucial Roe v. Wade Supreme Court decision assuring a woman's right to choose is in danger. Billions are made from exploiting women in the sex industry and throughout our culture. Violence against women is also closely connected with special oppression of women as a whole.

When public funds go to big developers rather than to affordable housing, education, health care and community facilities, women are impacted first, as they seek to fill their families' needs in these areas.

Since there is a gender gap in voting, reaction seeks to reduce the vote of women. The capitalists as a whole, or reaction in particular, either gain extra profits directly from the oppression or gain ground in the political arena, which then becomes an instrument for their enrichment.

Oppression of the LGBT community

The LGBT community continues to experience second-class con-stitutional rights, discrimination in marriage and family rights, on the job, in the military, in housing and everywhere else. They are victims of threats and physical abuse, including at the hands of the police, and suffer all kinds of insults in the media and culture. Who gains and loses from such treatment?

Relative and absolute impoverishment

The growing disparity between rich and poor here and around the world, and the growing absolute impoverishment of the bottom half of the U.S. population in recent years is caused by capitalism. Some 36 million people live below the poverty level. In the best of times offi-cial unemployment is around 4.5 percent, or over 5 million jobless, and during recessions as many as 7 to 8 million may be unemployed. The 25 percent jobless rate of the Great Depression of the 1930s can-not be ruled out. These constitute "the reserve army of the unem-ployed."

Capitalism has repeatedly promised to change the situation, but the necessity for maximum profit built into the system only makes mat-ters worse. Masses of people were impoverished under prior social systems but then, productive forces did not make it possible to pro-duce enough for everyone to have a good standard of living when goods are properly distributed.

Health

Now we have the means to prevent the spread of most diseases and to cure or contain many more. Yet such diseases as HIV-AIDS, malar-ia and tuberculosis kill millions in Africa and elsewhere because funds are lacking for prevention and treatment. Some 47 million people in the U.S. lack medical coverage. Even less coverage exists for family health services, elder care, mental health, etc.

Public funds that could assure universal medical coverage are used instead to pay for wars and military spending, and to provide many forms of subsidy to giant corporations. Insurance companies and other health profiteers siphon off funds that might otherwise provide health care for those who cannot afford it.

Other daily living needs

Society can now provide a quality education preschool through college, child care, affordable housing, and a livable environment. But these are missing or grossly under-funded because money from the unpaid labor of workers goes to wars and military spending, tax cuts for big corporations and the wealthy, and many other forms of subsidies to these modern-day robber barons.

Youth's needs

Youth under modern U.S. capitalism face the danger of having to serve as cannon-fodder, a completely uncertain job market, and inadequate education and job training. Recreational facilities and cultural programs are lacking. If anything, youth are seen as a challenge to the system or a criminal threat. It is not thought worthwhile to spend much money on youth since they are not yet steadily producing products and services through which capitalists acquire profit. Young workers often now face a two-tier wage system in which they are grossly discriminated against for equal work or work of comparable value. As a result, super profits are obtained from the labor of youth in such situations and the system is used to pit younger and older workers against each other.

Culture

Capitalism has converted culture into "commodities" produced by artists, whose labor is exploited to produce the maximum surplus value and resulting profit. If no profit is expected, that performer's effort is not undertaken or is cancelled. That is true whether the performer is part of a working-class neighborhood combo, a national recording star, or a classical music artist. In order to maximize profit, the artistic taste of as many people as possible is debased and commercialized.

Most talented artists of all kinds find it very hard to make a living from their art, and the great bulk of working people find it difficult to afford the quantity and quality of cultural activities they would like to enjoy. Performers who insist on humanistic content have an especially hard time earning a living, or even performing free for an audience, as commercialization is the key to capitalist financing.

Now let us examine how the capitalist economy works. Why does it create such ugly consequences for working people, the large major-

2 The Political Economy of Capitalism*

❖ The most essential features of a capitalist economy
❖ How Marx studied capitalism and discovered its laws of development
❖ The commodity, and commodity production
❖ Value, the labor theory of value, the law of value
❖ Labor as a commodity, surplus value, exploitation
❖ Profit and the rate of profit
❖ The average rate of profit
❖ The law of motion of capitalism: Drive for maximum surplus value and maximum profit
❖ Defining the working class and productive work
❖ The law of the tendency of the rate of profit to fall
❖ Absolute and relative impoverishment
❖ Reproduction of capital, inherent anarchy of production, the economic cycle
❖ Monopoly capitalism, imperialism and state monopoly capitalism
❖ Capitalist globalization: Transnational phase of the imperialist stage
❖ Financialization of capitalism
❖ The general crisis of capitalism theory

The most essential features of a capitalist economy

Under capitalism, the people who own the means of production and distribution are called the capitalist class. The other great class is the working class. Workers do not own means of production or distribution, such as factories or trucking companies. They possess only their own ability to work. To be able to live, the workers must sell their ability to work to the capitalist class. We shall see how their labor produces a greater value than that necessary to pay their wages. This extra value is called "surplus value," and is the source of capitalist profit and capital. All workers either work in the sphere of production of commodities and add new value, or in the sphere of the circulation of commodities. As we shall see, the unpaid labor of both categories of workers goes to capitalist class profit.

At Marx' graveside, Engels discussed Marx's two greatest scientific discoveries. In the next chapter, we will discuss the other great discovery, the role of the mode of production in the development of soci-

*See Glossary for explanation of the term "political economy."

ety. Here we begin with Marx' discovery of the law of motion of capitalism, which is that the capitalists do what is necessary to seek to maximize surplus value. Surplus value is the new value created by workers in the sphere of production over and above the value of the exercise of their labor power, which is more or less the amount of their wage. Because the capitalist owns the means of production, the product of the exercise of the worker's ability to work (labor power) which is above the wage is called the surplus value. It belongs to the capitalist as the source of profit.

This theory of surplus value and the law of motion of capitalism are at the heart of Marxism. They explain what the capitalists do to make profit and to accumulate capital from the exploitation of the worker. They explain why the working class wages a class struggle against the capitalist class and why the working class is the decisive class for social progress and must lead the struggle for socialism. The drive to maximize surplus value and profit underlies all the major social ills of capitalism, though in some cases through one or more mediations, or direct causes.

When capitalism is replaced, this law of motion—capitalists seeking to maximize surplus value—no longer operates because it exists only as an outgrowth of the specific class relation between capitalists and workers in the process of capitalist production. Extraction of surplus value from the unpaid labor of the working class ends with capitalism, permitting society to end forever many of the great social ills of capitalism.

Now we shall examine how Marx came to his theory of surplus value and its consequences.

How Marx studied capitalism
and discovered its laws of development

Even in Marx's day, capitalism was a very complex system. Marx used the method of scientific abstraction. He began by ignoring all of capitalism's complications. He looked for the simplest, least complicated expression of the essence of capitalist relations of production. This he found in the study of the commodity, and simple commodity production and exchange. He then uncovered more and more complexities of its development. His many years of historical study of how in fact capitalism developed confirmed his theoretical model.

The commodity, and commodity production

Marx found that a commodity had both some kind of use value to someone, and an exchange value—a value in an exchange between seller and buyer. A commodity is a product of labor made for exchange, either for another commodity or for money. If an individual makes a table for personal use, it is not a commodity, but if it is made to exchange for four chairs, or for $150, it is a commodity. When capitalist commodity production exists, the products of labor do not belong to the producer, the worker. Rather they belong to the owner of the means of production who, because of that ownership, also owns the products of labor and what they are exchanged for in money or products. The purpose of setting in motion the production of the commodity is to realize a surplus in the exchange. When this is the dominant form of production, capitalist production relations predominate. The capitalist economic system exists.

When an owner of the means of production—of the raw materials, tools, place to work, energy, etc.—hires a worker (who owns no means of production), to make a table or any other product for exchange at a gain, then this is capitalist commodity production.

Value, the labor theory of value, the law of value

Value, or exchange value, is the socially necessary labor time required to produce a commodity. The "socially necessary labor time" is the average amount of time it takes to produce the commodity. If it takes 8 hours on average to produce a certain type of table and 8 hours to produce four chairs, their value is the same and they should exchange for the same amount of money. Commodities exchange at their value, in proportion to the socially necessary labor time embodied in them. One table will exchange for 4 chairs, in our example, not for 1 chair or for 8 chairs. This law of value under capitalism appears as a gravitational center point around which every particular exchange of commodities varies somewhat from value but always tends toward it, due to the operation of the market and supply and demand. Supply and demand tend to be in balance when commodities exchange at equal values. Otherwise, if 1 chair could be exchanged for the price of 1 table, more chairs would be produced to benefit from the exchange, until the increased supply would drive the price of chairs down to the equivalent of 4 chairs for 1 table.

In nearly all classrooms where bourgeois economics is taught, the existence of the law of value is denied. Later we shall see why. Capitalist economics looks at the surface of things, and concludes that supply and demand determine price. It does not examine how the law of value brings about changes in supply and demand so that the result is that the price tends toward value as the basis of exchange. All of the "marginal analysis" used in bourgeois economics to explain the exact final behavior in economic decisions hides the role of value in compelling adjustments to conform to the law of value.

Labor as a commodity, surplus value, exploitation

Labor power is the ability of the worker to work and is what the capitalist buys when he or she hires the worker and pays wages. Since the worker owns no means of production and must be hired to live, he or she sells labor power to the capitalist. As a commodity, the value of labor power is the socially necessary labor time it takes to produce it (and reproduce it). This is the time it takes to produce the necessities of life to bring forward this type of labor power, including skill, education and family existence. Labor power becomes a commodity, with all the products of its exercise belonging to the capitalist. The worker is not paid for his or her work—for what is produced—but for the ability to labor over a period of time. The value of labor power changes according to historic conditions in a given country and among countries, as to what is "necessary" for labor of the particular kind to come forward. Its value expressed in money terms is the wage. Wages, however, can be below value, as when an African American worker is paid less than a white worker for the same expenditure of labor power, or African American and white workers in the South are paid less than African American and white workers in the North for similar work. A worker in an exceptionally strong union may be paid above value for a while.

The worker is hired or kept on only so long as he or she is able to produce more value than the value of the labor power expended in a day. That is, a surplus product created by the worker becomes surplus value that belongs to the capitalist simply because the capitalist owns the means of production. And therefore, the results of the worker's labor, including that part above the expenditure for the worker's labor power (or wage) goes to the capitalist. The capitalist has met his obligation by paying the value of the labor power expended (the wage).

Labor power is the only commodity whose use creates a value greater than the cost to maintain or produce it.

As a scientific economic concept, exploitation exists wherever a worker produces over and above the value of his or her own labor power, a surplus product or surplus value which belongs to the capitalist because of ownership of the means of production. The capitalist engages in commodity production to achieve a surplus which becomes profit or there is no reason to be a capitalist. The capitalist will not long stay in business unless he or she succeeds in realizing surplus value. Thus capitalist commodity production requires exploitation to exist. For part of the workday the worker produces the value equivalent to his or her wage, and the rest of the day the labor is "unpaid" surplus value to the capitalist.

The worker who works in what Marx termed the "productive" sphere—that is, where new commodities are produced—is thus exploited, since his or her unpaid labor allows the capitalist to realize surplus value. But it is also fair to say that in the sphere of the circulation of commodities, where most of what we now term "service" workers labor, their unpaid expenditure of labor power is also necessary for the capitalists in both the spheres of circulation and production to be able to realize a share of the surplus value produced in the productive sphere. The capitalist where computers are made must sell the computers at a price which allows the retailer of computers to pay the workers who do the work necessary to sell the computers and still allow the capitalist retailing them to reap a share of the surplus value created in the productive sphere, through the unpaid labor of workers in the circulation sphere. Thus it can be said that all workers are exploited, or they would not be hired. We will discuss the spheres of production and circulation more later.

The rate of exploitation is a comparison of the amount of surplus value realized by the capitalist for the expenditure of the worker's labor power, which usually equals the wages paid. Another way of expressing this comparison is to compare the s or surplus value achieved with the v or variable capital expended. Variable capital is what is paid for the expenditure of labor power, which is approximately the wage paid. The formula to express the comparison and establish the rate of exploitation is $s/v \times 100$.

Let us assume the furniture worker makes one table in a day which the capitalist sells for $150 and the worker is paid $30 for an 8 hour day. The total value of the table in money terms is $30 for materials and a part of the wearing out or using up of the tools, factory, etc. (called constant capital or "c"), plus $30 for wages, plus $90 in surplus value = $150. Leaving out of consideration for a moment the constant capital, "c", this means that if S, the surplus value, is $90 and V, the variable capital (value of labor power, wages), is $30 then the comparison or ratio of S to V is 3 to 1 or 300%

$$\text{rate of surplus value} = \frac{\text{surplus value}}{\text{variable capital or wages}} = \frac{S}{V} = \frac{90}{30} = \frac{3}{1} = 300\%$$

Thus 300% is the rate of exploitation or the rate of surplus value. For production as a whole, the rate of exploitation is 2 or 3 to 1 and slowly increases. The bourgeois "value-added" statistics give a rough idea of this quantity. Therefore, in the first 2 hours to 2 hours and 40 minutes of an 8 hour day the worker produces enough new value to pay his or her own wages, and for the rest of the day is producing surplus value for the capitalist, working for free.

The actual value of labor power and the amount paid in wages in specific cases can vary considerablyfor some time. Causes for this already mentioned include the super profits from racism generally, and the North-South wage differential; or, reflecting a very strong union, or the absence of any union. Monopolies can sometimes exert their economic and political power to buy constant and variable capital below value, and sell their products above value to realize a higher rate of exploitation and profit.

Lower wages for the same work, or work of comparable value, will result in the wages received being below the value of the labor power expended. Two-tier wage systems, which especially affect young workers, also result in wages for the lower tier that are below value.

In industrial production, a part of the surplus value extracted has to be shared with commercial capitalists for them to achieve their profit and pay their workers. Thus a direct translation of the value of labor power to wages paid is often only a rough approximation. But as we shall see in the discussion of the average rate of profit and the prices of production, there is always a tendency toward approximately equal value and price, or in this case, the value of labor power and wages paid.

Profit and the rate of profit

The capitalist considers the profit not only in terms of the surplus value gained compared to the expenditure on variable capital or wages, but also compared to the expenditure on constant capital (for objects of labor, instruments of labor, factory use, energy, etc.). Therefore, the rate of profit is the comparison (or ratio) of the surplus value created only by variable capital V, which is the expenditure for labor power, to the expenditure for all capital, constant and variable. Therefore the rate of profit = S (surplus value) divided by C+V (constant capital–materials, tools) + (variable capital) = $90/($30+$30) which is a ratio of 1.5 which is equivalent to a rate of profit of 150%.

$$\text{rate of profit} = \frac{\text{surplus value}}{\text{variable capital} + \text{constant capital (materials, tools, energy)}} = \frac{V}{V+C} = \frac{90}{30+30} = \frac{3}{2} = 150\%$$

Actually many economists today estimate the general rate of profit considering the economy as a whole as between 10 and 14%. The absolute amount of total capitalist profit has grown rapidly. In current estimates of profit, Marxists also need to take into account many other factors, and decide whether they are profits through the sphere of production or gains by the big monopolies in the sphere of circulation, or new and additional forms of variable or constant capital. These include taxes, advertising, bribes, luxuries charged to the corporations, bonuses, sales personnel, corporate cars, accountants, etc.

The average rate of profit

In different industries there are different rates of surplus value—exploitation—and different proportions of capital are spent on constant capital and wages. As a result there can be different rates of profit. But if there were substantially different rates of profit, capitalists would move into industries with the higher rates, increasing supply until the rate of profit is forced down, and leaving less supply in the former industries until the rates of profit went up. There is a resulting tendency to achieve a similar or average rate of profit throughout industry. Actually, two different average profit rates exist—one for monopolized industry and one for non-monopolized industries.

The law of motion of capitalism:
Drive for maximum surplus value and maximum profit

Does the capitalist have to drive for extracting maximum surplus value and realizing maximum profit? Why can't the capitalist be satisfied with "only" a "reasonable" profit and pay a "fair" wage? Does the capitalist not realize a profit by buying his input factors (wages, raw materials, machinery, factory, energy) cheap and selling the finished product high?

If every capitalist did the same thing—and most exchanges are between capitalists in which one is seller and the other buyer at different stages of production and circulation of commodities—then how would it be possible for the capitalist class as a whole to realize a profit?

Marx answered this by showing that in the process of production, the workers produce new value—a surplus value that belongs to the capitalist—or they would not be hired as workers, and this enables the capitalist class as a whole to realize a profit. The value of the commodity produced is the amount of socially necessary labor time contained in it. The worker is paid for the socially necessary labor time it requires to bring forth that kind of labor on average, and the capitalist keeps the surplus the worker creates over and above his or her wage.

It is true that all capitalists try to sell at prices higher than value because they have some kind of monopoly situation, or produce at a cost below value and sell at a little below value but sell a greater quantity. There are attempts to reap higher profit in the sphere of circulation as well, but as we saw in the discussion of the average rate of profit, this leads to shifts in production such that commodities tend to be exchanged at value. So over a period of time, there is no other source of surplus value and profit for the capitalists as a whole class than the unpaid labor of the working class.

Therefore, to extract more surplus value in order to realize more profit is the only way not only to "get ahead" of the competition, but to stay even, or to prevent being driven out of business.

To be "a nice guy" and not drive too hard for profit, not to drive your workers and exploit them "too hard," is to risk being driven out of business by present or possible future competitors, by bigger competitors who can lower prices temporarily until you are driven out of business. Over years in different parts of the country and different industries, the experience of the exceptional capitalist who tries to pay better wages and conditions is that "good guys come in last" and do not survive. If you achieve lower profits, you do not accumulate sufficient "reserves" for cyclical downturns, you are charged more by the bank as not as good a risk, suppliers' terms are more harsh, etc. Therefore, capitalism drives the capitalist to seek maximum profit, if that has not become the modus operandi from the very daily activity of being a capitalist.

To maximize profits requires maximizing the extraction of surplus value by speed-up, by extending the working day, by introducing more machinery and technology. But as we will discuss in the next section, improved technology and new materials, etc. while increasing the mass of surplus value, usually do not increase the rate of surplus value, and so become a treadmill that may actually reduce the rate of profit by increasing the organic composition of capital—more constant capital in relation to variable capital (wages).

Thus capitalism has an inherent character of constantly seeking to extract the maximum of surplus value in order to achieve the maximum profit. This is the underpinning of two things: the class struggle and the unmet needs of society. The capitalist class is driven to get more out of the workers for less in order to remain capitalists. The working class is driven by the requirements of living and the human desire for a better life, to resist this effort of the capitalists and to strive for higher wages and better conditions and benefits, so that the absolute amount and rate of exploitation is constantly reduced and finally eliminated entirely by eliminating the capitalist system that is built on it and requires it. This is the basis of the class struggle from the standpoint both of the working class and the capitalist class.

While the immediate cause of some of the great social ills is not the capitalist drive for maximum profits, the causes of those ills can be traced back through one or more mediations to this drive for maximum profit. Seeking the maximum of surplus value underlies the main directions capitalism develops under ever-changing conditions. It is the main determinant of the direction capitalist development takes. Therefore, to seek the maximum of surplus value (in order to realize maximum profit) is the law of motion of capitalism.

Defining the working class and productive work

For some years Marxist political economists tended to define the components of the working class narrowly. Some argued that only productive workers in the sphere of production belonged to the working class at all, or were important. A productive worker was one whose labor produced commodities and new value and was the source of surplus value. Commodities had to be material commodities, such as steel, cars, coal, or electronic products produced by workers in these industries. Those who worked for merchant capitalists in retail sales, in a department store or supermarket, were in the sphere of circulation of commodities. So were bank employees working for loan capitalists. But hospital workers, and restaurant and food workers, neither produced material commodities that could pass from hand to hand nor participated in the sphere of circulation.

But more careful study of Marx, especially "The Theories of Surplus Value," brought forth a different view. There, Marx gave examples of a teacher in a private school, an opera singer on salary and a tailor who worked for an employer. All produced services involving non-material commodities. The teacher and the opera singer produced non-material commodities—knowledge, and singing—that were consumed at the moment of production. These commodities were sold at value and embodied the realization of surplus value by the capitalist owner. The same analysis came to be accepted for hospital and other health care workers, food industry workers, etc. Thus the working class and its productive sector were greatly expanded.

Marx discussed transportation workers' role in bringing the necessary inputs for production, including the most important one—labor power—to the site of commodity production, and then bringing the commodities to the site of circulation. Marx treated the work of the transportation worker in both cases as productive work, as an extension of production off the site of production, work that without being performed would make the production process incomplete.

Marx also found that work done by workers in the entire sphere of circulation of commodities was necessary to realize surplus value in the sphere of production where commodities are produced, and new value and surplus value created. The unpaid labor of workers in the sphere of circulation was necessary for the whole capitalist class to realize a share of the surplus value created during production. Marx noted that full surplus value cannot be realized at the factory gate, but also required the retail counter.

Today, this analysis is extended to large numbers of workers in public employment, information, communications and many scientific fields. They, too, are new sections of the working class whether they produce material or non-material commodities or participate in the sphere of circulating commodities. It takes time for these newer sections of the working class to become fully, consciously integrated into the working class. Their addition makes the working class larger and even more diverse as to the work that is performed by its different strata. The U.S. working class now numbers well over 150 million people.

Public workers include several categories similar to those discussed. Some workers employed by a governmental entity produce physical commodities for sale, such as uranium. Some produce services for sale, such as licenses—non-material commodities which are a token of various rights. And some perform bureaucratic work necessary to keep the full circuit of activity under capitalism functioning so capitalists in all branches of the economy can reap a share of the surplus value created during production of material and non-material commodities.

Law of the tendency of the rate of profit to fall

The drive to maximize the extraction of surplus value from the working class and as a result to maximize profit is intensified by the tendency of the rate of profit to decline. How does this happen? When the portion of constant capital compared to variable capital (the organic composition) is high in a given industry in comparison with another industry, the rate of profit is lower. This is because the increased machinery and/or technology almost always enables an increase of surplus value less than that needed to offset the increase in the value of the additional constant capital. Usually, though, the absolute amount of profit is greater, since the total operation is usually bigger and employs many more workers, etc. The individual capitalist introduces new machinery/technology in order to produce more efficiently than other capitalists in the same line. And when the capitalist does so, he or she is able to produce the product at less than the socially necessary labor time, but sell it at value, which is the socially necessary labor time. Therefore, the individual capitalist secures extra surplus value until everyone else introduces the same kind of equipment and thereby reduces the socially necessary labor time and the value at which the commodity is generally sold.

The end result, then, is that the organic composition of this capital has been increased and the rate of profit is decreased, while the absolute amount of profit grows. This is only a tendency, because it can be offset for a period of time by such things as speedup, extending the workday (overtime), reducing health care, etc., which may well increase extraction of surplus value sufficiently to offset the increase in constant capital—the machinery newly introduced. But the treadmill that drives the capitalists to strive for maximum surplus value and resulting maximum profit is unavoidable.

Absolute and relative impoverishment

Marx found there was a law of the tendency toward absolute impoverishment of the working class, and also a law of the relative impoverishment of the working class. The drive inherent in capitalism to maximize the extraction of surplus value to realize maximum profit, and the tendency of the rate of profit to decline, help explain why the working class suffers from relative and even absolute impoverishment. Such impoverishment can be seen in a given country, or in the world as a whole. Such a process is evident, especially for the bottom half of the working class by income or wealth, as compared to the top few percent of the capitalists, or just the top few hundred of the world's richest capitalists. The disparity grows continuously and is only temporarily offset to some extent. Several hundred of the wealthiest capitalists possess more than do a third to half of the people of the world. The law of motion of capitalism results in such continual relative impoverishment.

Concerning absolute impoverishment, whole countries in Africa, Asia and the Americas and sections of the population of others experience the tendency toward absolute impoverishment over long stretches of time. This is the "law of the tendency" because countervailing tendencies are also inherent in capitalism, and which one predominates at a particular time requires specific study. While there are contradictory tendencies, the value of labor power tends to go up as modern society requires higher educational standards for the worker and his or her family, and other factors of history and culture require higher living standards in absolute terms. There is also the growth of the labor movement, and of its success in fighting for higher wages and working conditions.

Reproduction of capital,
inherent anarchy of production, the economic cycle

The capitalist system requires continual reproduction of capital on an ever-expanding basis. But private capitalist ownership of the means of production and distribution means anarchy of production. The huge economy requires a high level of integration, as well as proportions among the productive sector and the sphere of circulation and among all their subparts such that they mesh and have proper portions at the right time. Private ownership does not permit such proportionate development.

Some claim Marxism has no theory of the business or economic cycle. But Marx discusses the four phases of the cycle, why they are inherent in capitalism, why they come into existence and what role they play in the capitalist economy. The cycle begins with the boom phase. In this phase, it appears the capitalists can expand production and sales without limit. Each capitalist expands to grab a bigger piece of what is seen as an ever-expanding market, without fully knowing what competitors are doing. Such expansion produces a potential for a big disproportion between supply and demand, which at some point takes place, and causes relative overproduction. This is not overproduction relative to the needs of working people. It is relative overproduction compared to the possibilities of effective demand, and profit, at that point. It is not a matter of under-consumption, as some, including on the left, characterize Marx's theory of the economic cycle. Marx points out that relative overproduction is realized and produces a crisis (the crisis phase) at a time when consumption is still rising. The crisis point marks the moment at which the capitalists, realizing the situation, try to restore an equilibrium between production and consumption by decreasing production. But each cut in production itself feeds a decline in consumption, because the cuts in production themselves reduce the possibility of consumption. As laid-off workers buy less, the result is further decline, and the expectation of still further decline.

In the depression phase of the cycle, capitalists attempt to put production and consumption back in proper relations with each other by finding ways to cut costs of production. This may include replacing

workers with new equipment, or closing some factories. But this causes more unemployment, and slows getting production and consumption back in line with each other. Finally, such attempts begin to produce recovery by placing production more in line with a new rising
demand that comes as replacement of equipment outstrips layoffs. The
recovery finally reaches a new boom period in which demand outstrips production and gives rise to the anticipation of further growth in
demand and production.

At all stages of the capitalist business cycle, there are many harmful social consequences.

During the crisis, depression and even the recovery phase, these
include the waste of workers' labor skills, mass joblessness, poverty,
unsaleable goods. The boom phase brings shortages and inflation of
the price of necessities.

No two economic cycles are alike. In recent years the cycle continues, but has changed considerably. The world capitalist economy is
now much bigger and much more closely intertwined. The cycle runs
its course in less time—now five to 10 years. It has been less profound,
with smaller, shorter contractions. It takes more in this size economy
to throw the whole into deep depression. Different stages of the cycle
can occur in different areas of the world, offsetting the disproportions.
Countercyclical actions conducted with the huge resources available
to the International Monetary Fund and World Bank, joint action of
the G-8 powers, or actions of the U.S. in managing its budget, and
through the activity of the Federal Reserve Bank, can postpone or ease
the effects of the cycle. But a depression on the scale of the Great
Depression of 1929 is by no means ruled out. There are limits on
international planning, even by giant transnationals, under the new
forms of private ownership of the means of production and distribution. The world economy is now so much more interlinked that disproportions in one financial center can also spread rapidly and get out of
control. If anything, capitalism is now a more unstable, volatile world
system. At present we are entering one of the deepest recessions since
the Great Depression. Finance capital has become even more dominant than Lenin predicted, and the current crisis began in the financial
sector connected to reckless housing profiteering.

Monopoly capitalism, imperialism
and state monopoly capitalism

The capitalist system as a whole develops through different stages. Each is still based on the findings, including laws of existence and development, first spelled out in Marx' "Capital." But the way these laws operate does change. What leads to changes and new laws is first and foremost development of the means of production. This then leads to changes in the forms of capitalist property ownership or in the relations of production within the framework of capitalism. "Free competitive" capitalism as it existed prior to the late 19th and early 20th centuries has developed into monopoly capitalism, with the economy and political life of the main European powers, the U.S., Japan and some other countries becoming dominated by great monopolies in various forms

Lenin gave the basic analysis of this new monopoly stage of capitalism in "Imperialism, the Highest Stage of Capitalism." He found the following five characteristics produced the new stage: 1) concentration and centralization of capital and production to the point where monopolies dominate the economy; 2) merger of industrial and banking capital, creating finance capital with a dominant financial oligarchy; 3) the export of capital along with the export of commodities becomes decisive; 4) division of the world economically by the monopolies; 5) territorial division of the world among the biggest monopoly capitalist powers is completed, and struggle for redivision takes place.

Lenin concluded from this that world wars and other wars to divide and redivide the world would be inevitable. Such imperialist aggression was not just a governmental policy. It was the new, monopoly capitalist or imperialist, stage of development of capitalism. This was a stage of wars and revolution, an epoch of the transition from capitalism to socialism. This was the final stage of capitalism, as well as its highest stage of development. It was parasitic, and decaying and moribund, but still capable of development and would not collapse of its own. It would have to be pushed off the stage of history. It would have a built-in tendency toward a more reactionary political direction. As we shall see, fascism in the world in the 1920s-1945, McCarthyism in the U.S., from 1947-1960s, and ultra-right reaction from the 1980s to the present, expresses the political tendency toward the right that

Lenin predicted. War to redivide the world among the imperialist powers is no longer considered inevitable, mainly due to the likelihood that it would involve world nuclear war, potentially destroying all humanity and all property. Such war, however, cannot be excluded as a possibility. Regional wars with more limited imperialist objectives evidently remain quite possible despite world peace sentiment and activity.

In connection with the development of the imperialist stage, Lenin developed the theory of just and unjust wars. He found that all imperialist wars were unjust, and therefore should be opposed. World War I, being an imperialist war for redivision of the world, was unjust on all sides. The aim was to oppose it, and where possible to transform it into a revolutionary struggle to replace capitalism. A war for national independence against an invading or occupying imperialist power was a just war, to be supported. In a colony or a multinational country like Russia or Austria-Hungary, an oppressed nation had the right to fight for its freedom as a new nation-state, or if a nationality or a people, for full equality and compensatory treatment within the old state formation. But the choice was to be made by the oppressed people as a whole through their most representative leading organization(s), not by individuals or small grouplets.

With the development of atomic weapons and other weapons of mass destruction and of conventional weapons capable of killing millions in hours, those exercising the right of decision in a just war situation needed to take into account what would be appropriate means of conducting the liberation struggle from the standpoint of the interests of their own people, neighboring people and world humanity; and what means were capable of victory. There were now situations in which the military balance was so overwhelmingly negative that independence through military means was not possible and their use, in that sense, was no longer just, though the struggle through all other means and with full international support was just. The international community has now also concluded that an otherwise just struggle cannot be conducted by military action against civilians, or with disregard for civilian casualties. Such military action itself is unjust.

Within the imperialist stage, capitalism develops a new phase called the state monopoly capitalist phase. This represents a fusion of the economic and political power of the state and monopolies on a qualitatively new level, in which the state becomes a major direct vehicle for exploitation, for the realization and distribution of surplus value. Another purpose for state monopoly capitalism is to use the state to ameliorate to some degree the social ills of capitalism, so that the system is relatively stabilized, and less subject to sharp opposition from the working class and its allies. Lenin described state monopoly capitalism as the completion of the material preparation for progressing to socialism.

Capitalist globalization:
Transnational phase of the imperialist stage

In the 1960s the means of production grew rapidly in terms of computerization, communication, transportation, and new materials that made possible and necessary a qualitative turn in the internationalization of economic life. For capitalism to fully utilize these developments, and make possible the further enrichment of capital based on these advances in the means of production, the relations of production of capitalism were modified so that transnational monopolies in industrial production, banking, merchandizing, conglomerates and combinations of these became dominant in the 1970s and 80s. Some 300 such transnationals based in the U.S. became dominant in the world, often intertwined with another 300 or so based in the other major imperialist powers.

At a moment's notice the transnationals could transmit billions and trillions of dollars anywhere in the world; cut production in one country and increase it in their plants in many other countries; deplete manufacturing of some products in the U.S., shift their production to other countries and then import them back into the U.S. for sale, making extra profits that way. They could pit steel workers in U.S.-based transnational companies against steel workers in giant Brazilian-based companies, etc. They could decide on their own or together with other transnationals—with whom they sometimes competed— which countries would produce which lines of products, which would distribute them and which would consume them, all from the standpoint of maximizing profits. They had such power and were so intertwined with governments that they could create maximum tax loopholes, and move capital off-shore, or anywhere in the world.

These developments are giving rise to new forms of unions in different countries working together against the same company or industry, including the formation of truly international unions—one union in the same industry for a number of countries.

The term "globalization" has become popular. It is loosely used to cover all these developments. "Globalization" has different definitions according to one's class and political orientation. For Marxists, there are aspects of the new developments which are objective, that result primarily from very big changes in the forces of production— in information, communication and control technology, transportation, etc.—that bring about internationalization of economic life on a totally new scale and basis. But how this is organized and used, for what aims, and its impact on the workers and other popular masses of all countries, depends on whether it is done under capitalism or social-ism.

Capitalist globalization develops through further qualitative change in the existing monopoly capitalist, imperialist stage of capitalism. "Globalization" is a new phase of monopoly capitalism in which the main characteristics of the imperialist stage undergo further qualitative changes, but without losing their overall character. The monopolies undergo further combinations of capital into giant transnationals—each located in many countries—whether a financial, industrial, or commercial transnational or some combination of these types. The change in form is to maximize capitalist profit-making through full use of the new means of production that enable rapid shifts in funds, production, and merchandizing around the world to take advantage of cheaper labor and all other factors of profit, and by pitting workers of one country against others to force maximum concessions in wages, work standards and benefits.

Now it takes only several hundred such transnational corporations based in the U.S., Japan, Germany, the U.K., etc. to dominate the whole world capitalist economy. These transnationals also intertwine with one or more national states to achieve their goals. But it would be wrong to conclude that the transnationals have now replaced the big imperialist states and that these states now play no role in the world except as directed by a particular transnational. The transnationals both combine for given purposes and fight one another to compete for maximum profit. What particular interests dominate in the economically, politically and militarily powerful countries is a reflection not only of the unity and competition of the transnationals, but of the total balance of forces, including the role of political parties and their mass base, and the status of democracy in the given country. Certainly, the Bush administration's role in world developments cannot be reduced simply to that of a puppet of one or more transnationals. However, the transnationals—and the particulars of their character and functioning—play a new and highly significant role in the policies of the U.S. administration and those of the other imperialist powers.

This is the phase of the monopoly capitalist stage, in which internationalization of economic life and the dominance of the transnational monopolies—capitalist globalization—has become decisive. It requires a completely new internationalism on the part of the working class and popular forces of all countries if they are to protect their living standards and interests and succeed in advancing them. Every step becomes crucial in building truly international unions, in joint contract negotiations, in international regulation and control of the movement of capital in the interests of the working people.

Financialization of capitalism

Within the basic framework of the monopoly capitalist stage of capitalism and its state monopoly capital and transnational monopoly (globalization) phases, a new qualitative change has taken place. That change is now called financialization. The changes in the 1960s and 1970s that brought into existence the growth and dominance over the world capitalist economy by a small number of transnational monopoly corporations set in motion the forces that produced financialization. Globalization required and made possible the growth of banks, investment houses and similar financial institutions that were transnational in scope, to finance the growth of transnational industries, commercial and other corporations. The non-financial transnationals set the pace in moving away from obtaining maximum profits by providing new or superior products at lower costs and marketing products in a superior fashion. Instead the tendency was to shift production rapidly between countries according to the bottom line results. As former General Motors head Charles Wilson once said, "We are in the business of making money, not of making cars."

In Lenin's day, he spoke of monopoly capitalism producing a merger of banking and industrial capital into finance capital in which banking capital became dominant and produced a financial oligarchy. He also predicted that process would lead to an increasingly reactionary political direction for capitalism. In those days, the dominant financial interests were still interested in using their bank capital to realize greater profits extracted from the workers in the process of production of industrial products and from raw material and similar commodities.

In recent years financial domination aimed to separate itself from direct involvement with industrial and commercial capital and seek maximum profits from the financial sector with little direct connection to manufactured and constructed commodities and raw materials, and so on. The aim of such separation and domination, called "financialization, was by nature much more parasitic and speculative, ponzi schemes, as little connected to the "real" economy as possible. Mortgages on homes, apartments, offices and other large construction projects were bundled together and converted into securities to be bought and sold at higher and higher prices in great gambles.

Whereas previously the immediate cause of an economic crisis was relative overproduction of physical commodities in the process of seeking maximum profits under conditions of anarchy of production, financialization brings relative overproduction of financial products such as securities in conditions of anarchy of their production. When cyclical relative overproduction of housing was reached and a pull-back began, the financial products backed by mortgages forced a sudden large pull-back from the financial products based on the mortgages. There was relative overproduction of the financial products themselves. Such overproduction was aggravated by the much greater risk-taking that had grown up due to deregulation of financial institutions enacted by the executive and legislative branches of government and championed by those closest to Wall Street. New risky financial institutions like hedge funds came into existence as did risky new financial instruments such as credit default swaps and other derivatives. Together all these expressions of financialization of the economy produced a financial and economic crisis that began in December 2007 with a recession and in September 2008 with a financial panic that quickly spread around the world, reflecting globalization. The biggest banks, investment houses, insurance companies and other financial institutions, most based in the U.S., were on the verge of bankruptcy and some failed. The Bush administration and the Democratic-dominated Congress moved rapidly to bail them out with

$700 billion, half of which was immediately distributed, but without any real restrictions or directions for the use of these huge sums.

The crisis has now spread throughout the world and to all sectors of the U.S. economy and constitutes the most profound crisis since the Great Depression of the 1930s. Ten million are already jobless and 10 million families face loss of their foreclosed homes. While providing the hundreds of billions to Wall Street, the most reactionary section of the Republicans tried unsuccessfully to block a $17 billion-plus bridge loan to the U.S. auto companies. The loan has conditions pressuring the United Automobile Workers (UAW) to make still more concessions to the companies, though they already made major concessions in the last two contracts. Faced with the choice of losing a total of 3 million or more jobs with a closing of the auto companies, the unions and workers were reluctantly compelled to support a bailout for the auto companies with conditions. What remains to be seen during the Obama administration is how much more of a bailout will be necessary, what conditions will be imposed for higher environmental and other social goals, and whether the bailout with conditions will keep the auto companies and the auto workers' jobs going.

Economists predict the crisis will last three to five years before a recovery ends it. Some suggest the U.S. may face the situation the Japanese did not so long ago of a 10- year recession. The Obama administration which will soon take office promises as its first priority a large stimulus package costing $500-700 billion, to benefit "Main Street" and give a shock to the economy that gets it going again. This would include public works projects such as jobs building bridges, repairing roads, sewage systems, school buildings, providing insulation for housing and buildings, electronic updating of schools, and green jobs. The package would also include expansion of unemployment compensation, food stamps and aid to state and city governments, and provisions to protect homes from foreclosure. Re-regulation of financial institutions is also proposed.

Re-regulation and some of the other proposals of the Obama administration make less likely an early repetition of the present financial and economic crisis. However, financialization is now an objective process of the developed monopoly capitalist system especially in its globalization phase. It is centered in the United States at least as long as U.S. imperialism is still top dog in the world.

Financialization and its consequences can no more be entirely avoided than can the economic cycle and its periodic crises, even though no crisis duplicates any previous one. The financial interests that now dominate U.S. capitalism see a future only for the financial sector and satellite industries. They are satisfied to deindustrialize the U.S. even more, leaving only some research and development, military and energy industries, and industries to serve tourists and the rich. They expect only themselves to be in control. Not long after the recovery, the financial interests will again attack government regulation and similar schemes will reemerge. The arguments about the hidden hand of capitalist competition working its magic and producing the model economy will reemerge. Government intervention will again be attacked as interfering with this magic and producing bad results.

But the periodic crises that capitalism reproduces lead to a growing recognition by millions that government partial and complete nationalization is necessary in a way that benefits them, not the big financial and other monopoly interests, and this leads to a recognition of the necessity of socialism if they are to have protection from economic crises and all the other ills produced by capitalism.

The general crisis of capitalism theory

Lenin characterized the present epoch as one of war and revolution, and the world transition from capitalism to socialism. During the leadership of Joseph Stalin, the theory of the general crisis of capitalism was developed. While it acknowledged there were and could be momentary setbacks in one country or another, it proclaimed that socialism in the USSR was irreversible, and that was then repeated in other socialist countries. In this view, a general crisis was taking place in all aspects of life under capitalism, and in all its major expressions—the developed capitalist countries, the colonies and the then-developing world. In the socialist world, it found smooth, crisis-free development in all aspects of life, from one stage forward to another.

This theory found different stages of a generally deepening crisis of capitalism, and a strengthening of the progressive forces in the world. The first stage was the victory of socialism in Russia. The second stage was in the defeat of fascism in World War II and the breakaway from capitalism of countries in Eastern Europe and Mongolia. The third stage was in the 1950s, when the colonial system was ended and the Chinese (1949) and Cuban (1959) revolutions won out. The deepening of the general crisis was examined in each stage in terms of the world capitalist economy, the political situation and ideological developments.

The world Communist movement concluded that the world balance of forces overall shifted in the 1960s when the USSR reached one-third of total U.S. production and the socialist countries together reached two-thirds of the capitalist world production. According to documents of the world Communist movement, the world balance of forces had reached the point that when the socialist countries, the national liberation movement and the working class and peace movement in the developed capitalist countries united, they were capable of preventing any particular war and determining the main direction of world social development, though temporary setbacks were still possible. There was discussion that a fourth stage of the general crisis had been reached by the mid-1970s with a sizable recession in the capitalist world, the new characterization being that capitalism had become so unstable that it could no longer achieve partial, temporary stabilization.

This estimate of world development proved to be simplistic and too optimistic. The fall of the Soviet Union and socialism in Eastern Europe and Mongolia came as a shock. There had been an underestimation of the reserves of capitalism, and its ability to achieve forms of relative stability, to grow and develop even in the midst of its internal contradictions, partial setbacks and instability. But capitalism could advance in some respects despite such blows as its defeat in Vietnam.

U.S. imperialism's ability to engage Serbia and Yugoslavia, to conduct the first Gulf War and the wars in Afghanistan and Iraq showed that the world peace forces were not yet strong enough to prevent such developments, though we now see the cost U.S. imperialism is paying for its aggression in Iraq and Afghanistan. On the other hand, the claim that socialism was irreversible in the USSR and other socialist countries of Europe proved wrong, as socialism proved much weaker than expected and was replaced by capitalist regimes.

We shall discuss this problem further in Chapter 4 on Socialism. But there is no reason to replace the old general crisis theory with a new one. There is no reason to think we will go through uniform general world stages of increasing deepening of the crisis of capitalism and the strengthening of socialism and the progressive forces. The transition from capitalism to socialism will happen, but it will not be nearly so neat as we had imagined, and there will be many ups and downs. The "ups" will be extremely diverse, both in the road taken and in what is achieved.

It remains true that capitalism has fundamental contradictions that cannot be completely overcome, but alongside such developments, world capitalism continues to have considerable reserves to keep it going, and to recover from setbacks. The deep-going contradictions of capitalism can change their forms, but they cannot be fundamentally eliminated or overcome. They do have a long-term tendency to deepen and become more intractable, but the picture is very complicated and uneven. It is now much more difficult to make reliable predictions of the concrete path of capitalist economic development. Information that once was public is now hidden by the transnationals and the governments they dominate.

The triumphalism of the capitalist political world at the collapse of the Soviet Union has already proved unwarranted. Capitalism's deep-going problems have resurfaced, and are leading to new radical trends in all areas of the world, and especially in Latin America.

Such features of capitalism remain and develop as: The absolute and relative exploitation of the working class is at an unprecedented level and continues to grow rapidly. Each transnational corporation now exploits not only its own employed workers in many countries and the entire working class of its home country. It now exploits the entire working class of the world. At the same time, the working class is growing both domestically and worldwide in numbers and in political maturity.

The movement of capital around the world in search of maximum profit is ever faster, whether in terms of the location of production, the supply of raw materials and other resources, research and development, mass distribution, location of finance capital, currency, or price manipulation and speculation.

Disproportions spread in the world's highly interdependent economy, and are harder to control because of the transnationals' dominance. Regulation by any single country has less effect. In some cases international trade agreements even override national sovereignty in favor of the transnationals. Economies are therefore more vulnerable to supply and currency manipulation. Relative overproduction while millions starve, and gross trade and currency imbalances, are among the chronic disproportions in the world capitalist economy. The result is greater instability and volatility, and more frequent economic cycles with attendant hardships at the bottom of the cycle, as well as prolonged stagnation. Therefore, the contradiction between the increasingly intertwined social character of production and distribution on the one hand, and the concentration of capital among fewer and fewer on the other hand, sharpens economic and social problems and contradictions. It also sharpens the class struggle and propels ever-wider sections of potential allies of the working class into democratic struggle at its side.

The advance of the means of production connected with the globalization of economic and social life under domination of the transnational monopolies requires a much higher level of environmental protection, education, health care, culture, housing and family care to produce the quantity and quality of labor now needed. This is in contradiction to the greater quantities of capitalist profit needed to sustain the growth of the giant transnationals, which can come only from high rates of exploitation of existing workers, and from the growing exploitation of workers worldwide. Intensification of the class struggle and sharper attacks on the living conditions of the working class are inherent in the dominance of the transnationals. The increasing merger of the transnationals with the state in the main capitalist countries means that capitalist globalization is both an economic and a political process—one which increases the danger of wars and is very damaging and degrading to the environment.

At the same time, and in reaction to such developments, the size, maturity and active struggle of the working class and the democratic forces as a whole—in their hundreds of millions—grows everywhere. In an uneven process, the worldwide movement is moving leftward again.

3 Historical Materialism

❖ The subject matter of historical materialism
❖ Social consciousness depends on social being
❖ The socioeconomic formation
❖ The mode of production
❖ Base and superstructure
❖ The state
❖ Non-superstructural aspects of society
❖ Human community: The national question
❖ U.S. nationality developments
❖ The class struggle
❖ The class struggle and the democratic struggle

To understand why the huge social problems of capitalism exist and how they came into being, and whether they can be cured under capitalism, it is necessary to study not only the political economy of capitalism. It is also necessary to know what role the capitalist economic system plays in capitalist society as a whole and how and why the capitalist economy and society developed, according to what laws and with what prospects for the future. Thus we must understand the subject matter of historical materialism.

The subject matter of historical materialism

Historical materialism studies how society develops, its laws and regularities of development. The Marxist study of history is a different but related subject. In the study of history, we examine why a particular event took place. Why did the Union Army win the battle of Gettysburg? Or we examine why something took place over a period of time. Why did slavery exist for such a long time in the U.S.? What were the immediate and more remote causes of a given historic event?

Historical materialism studies how the different aspects of society relate to one another, which aspect has more influence on the others, and whether directly or through one or more intermediary aspects (mediations) of society. Which aspects of social development are unique to a particular socioeconomic formation, which are common to all class societies and which to all social formations? How does one socioeconomic formation develop into another? Is there a particular sequence of such social formations? Are there variations, and why?

Are there laws and regularities of social development? After all, social development takes place through the activities of millions of people exercising their free will according to their varying desires, ideas and interests. For those who deny laws and regularities, social development is a result of the will and actions of great figures such as kings or generals, a result entirely of accident, or the result of unknown and unknowable forces. But Marx, Engels and Lenin argued that human beings do not decide on and produce their own desired world in a vacuum. They inherit conditions that shaped the world. That world shapes their class and personal interests and conscious-ness. The existing world places definite limits on people's desires and on the results of their activity. So both in setting and reaching goals, the process is fundamentally shaped by existing society.

Reflecting different details of the conditions of existence of indi-viduals and more substantial differences of the conditions of existence of different classes, people have conflicting desires for the outcome of their activity. Therefore, there are conflicts in what people seek and in the outcome of their actions. But because of the common reality shared by all in its large dimensions, and despite individual differ-ences, that general reality shapes what we set out to accomplish and also determines in large measure what it is actually possible to accom-plish. Thus the broad objective necessities present in the world we inherit are able to express themselves through all the accidents of the free will of millions.

Social consciousness depends on social being
Like all objective reality in nature and society, broad regularities or laws inherent in the current reality limit what can develop out of the present circumstances. It is also important to understand that exis-tence shapes consciousness, not the other way around. Even with "free will," social existence develops with inherent regularities. What are those regularities or laws?

Historical materialism studies all sides of society, recognizing that all aspects are interconnected and influence all others. But they do not influence each other equally. Some aspects influence others much more, and more directly. Some influence other aspects only indirectly, through one or more levels of mediation of other aspects. But laws of development in society never appear in pure form. They always appear in different, accidental, chance particulars, never twice the exact same way.

A law in social development asserts a regularity exists connecting one circumstance with another. Since the development of nuclear weapons and other ways to destroy all life on our planet, every law asserts as a first condition that if there is social development and A takes place, then B will take place. All social development requires some human activity. Will that activity bring into existence B as a result of the existence of A? Here we have an assumption of another law, that consciousness tends toward correspondence with objective reality and necessity. But that tendency can be held back and partially derailed for a period of time—sometimes a very long time—by class forces acting in accordance with their class interests to derail it.

Preventing consciousness from coming to correspond to objective reality happens when the ruling class controls information and communications and puts forward false consciousness. But with time, trial and error, use of Marxism and the building of Marxist organizations to reveal the real interests of the working class and its allies, those laws will ultimately operate more or less fully. As Abraham Lincoln said, "You can fool some of the people all of the time and all of the people some of the time, but you cannot fool all of the people all of the time."

What are some of the laws and theories of social development we shall examine?

Social consciousness depends on social being. If that is so, then we look for the source of the really big societal ills in the conditions of existence of people, not in ideas people have about society. Poverty is not a figment of some people's imagination. It exists as one expression of social being. When we recognize the existence of poverty, our ideas correspond to the existence of that part of social reality.

All aspects of society taken together constitute a particular socioeconomic formation, an integrated, interdependent system such as the ancient slave, the feudal, the capitalist and the socialist socioeconomic formations. A common capitalist socioeconomic formation exists even though any two countries will have significant differences, one from the other. To understand the causes of the big social problems it is necessary to study both the system as a whole and its most decisive aspects.

The mode of production plays the most important role in the development of the socioeconomic formation and the change from one formation to another.

The mode of production is the way in which people produce the necessities of life such as food, clothing, shelter—a list that continually expands. To be able to produce such necessities, two aspects of the mode of production are needed, the forces of production and the relations of production—how people relate to one another in the process of production. The relations of production are also class or property relations. Property relations deal with who owns the main means of production during each socioeconomic (social) system. During ancient slave society, the master owns the main productive property, human slaves. During feudalism, the lord owns the land with the serf tied to it, and during capitalism, the capitalist owns the means of production and distribution. These are the forms of property needed for profitable social production. (We are not talking here of personal household property.)

The forces of production are the other aspect of the mode of production. They consist of workers and their historically determined level of skill and the means of production. The means of production consist of the objects of labor and the means of labor. This latter consists of the instruments of labor, factories, energy, etc.

The most basic law of a socioeconomic formation and particularly of its mode of production is the law of the necessary correspondence of the relations of production to the level and character of the productive forces. When the relations of production get out of sync with the new forces of production because the dominant class prevents them from adjusting, all kinds of social problems develop. Such nonconformance of the relations of production (the class or property relations) to the forces of production is the basic contradiction that develops in class-divided societies.

The theory of base and superstructure shows how the dominant superstructure of a given socioeconomic formation defends the economic property base that exists. And such defense is a more immediate source of many major social ills. In the superstructure, the state plays a special role in defending the dominant property relations in the base. Different types of state, including the fascist type, present different orders of social catastrophe for masses of working people.

There are aspects of a socioeconomic formation that are neither part of the base or superstructure themselves but are closely related to the base and superstructure. The laws of physical sciences are in this category, but the products of science, like atomic weapons, can play a big role in the superstructure. Among the most important of the non-superstructural elements of the socioeconomic formation are the forms of human community that have developed. Today that includes the nation, nationality, or people. And given the capitalist base and a dominant superstructure that serves it, national and racial oppression becomes a prime instrument both of its super profits and its political domination. Therefore, we deal with the "national question" at some length, including an examination of how the national question has developed and is developing in the United States.

Once the main aspects of a socioeconomic formation are studied as to their relative importance and interactions and what great social problems emerge from them under capitalism, the question arises: What is the source of development of the socioeconomic formation, internally and from one formation to another? Marxism answers, the "class struggle." On the one hand, the class struggle aims to overcome the major social problems when that struggle is advanced by the exploited and oppressed to end such oppression with a new system. But the class struggle as pursued by the class trying to hold onto the old property relations and prevent change creates more social hardship for the masses of working people, by narrowing democratic rights and other means. But to understand how one socioeconomic formation can be replaced by a more advanced one, it is necessary to study and understand the role of the class struggle and its closely intertwined companion, the democratic struggle, as the engines of progress in social development.

That study brings us to understand the objective processes that both underlie the huge social ills the masses of people face under capitalism and show why the capitalist system is the source, cannot be fixed and needs to be replaced by socialism.

The laws of social development operate independently of whether particular people are aware of them. Their existence is part of objective reality.

They are all expressions of objective necessity and inevitability in social development. When necessity expresses itself, it is only in and through chance or accident, never in a universal form alone, never twice exactly the same way. The expression of inevitability in social development is only through human activity. In many situations this inevitability is expressed only after sharp struggle for higher levels of consciousness and activity and in strong competition with the class opponent. The outcome of a particular episode may be unclear, and in that sense not at all inevitable.

Some Marxists have argued as if Marxism allows us to predict the outcome of all or the most important struggles because the outcome is "inevitable" and the necessary consciousness, organization and strength come into being automatically as a result of some rigid determinism, without conscious struggle, and win out in every concrete situation as a matter of inevitability. This is a distortion of Marxism, a rigid determinism that in fact leads to the error of "voluntarism"—that if we wish it, it will happen, because it is already inevitable.

To say that so long as there is capitalism, there will be a class struggle of the working class against the capitalist class, is to state a law inherent in capitalism—a very important law to know. "The class struggle is inevitable under capitalism" is another way to put it. But that inevitability does not tell you how the class struggle will express itself, what its forms will be at a particular moment, when and at what level of commitment and consciousness it will occur, nor the outcome of each particular struggle and the balance of forces. None of those things are inevitable or matters of laws of social development. The necessity of class struggle takes place only through the accidents or chance occurrences that arise in the course of particular social developments, which are not inevitable.

The particular course of development that takes place is a matter of chance or accident in relation to the law of social development or necessity to which it gives expression. It is not chance or accident as it relates to the specific causes and effects of the actual course of development that takes place. The specific developments, however, are not predictable simply because the law exists, nor can they be predicted at a considerable distance. When you get close to an event, it is sometimes possible to predict the outcome of a social struggle, such as a strike. That can sometimes be possible when all the factors of the immediate balance of forces are clear.

Marx predicted the Communards of Paris in 1872 would lose in their effort to carry out the first working-class revolution to replace capitalism. He admired their heroic attempt but estimated that in view of the concrete relationship of forces and stage of development of the working class in France and of capitalism, it was too early in history to be able to win.

Yet Marx spoke of the "inevitability" that socialism would replace capitalism through the leadership of the working class. There was a necessity in capitalism that would compel the working class to struggle against the capitalist class and to seek to replace its dominant position with working-class leadership in the construction of socialism. There was a necessity in social development that the working class and its allies would win out, but when and under what circumstances was not predictable from a distance. And how many times it might be attempted and defeated because of particular chance circumstances could also not be predicted.

Yet every struggle also expressed immediately accidental factors of how the relationship of forces shaped up. These included the level of class consciousness and organization. But with detailed knowledge of such factors close to the time of decision, the outcome well might be predictable. Thus Marxism is a philosophy that considers determinism and indeterminism as implying the existence of each other, and is neither a determinist or indeterminist philosophy.

Necessity does not rule out surprises or anomalies. In fact it presumes them. Necessity can never exhibit itself in a pre-fixed way, only in the chance circumstances of a concrete path of development from many chance events. When such a path is full of chance circumstances coming together, we often consider it a surprise or an anomaly. It is also possible that more than one aspect of necessity is asserting itself in the same situation, but in conflicting directions as to outcome. Marx, in the political economy of capitalism, often talks about the law of the tendency for such and such to happen, such as for the rate of profit to decline with the growth of the organic composition of capital. But he then says this is only a tendency because there are other tendencies that run counter to it and the outcome of opposing tendencies cannot be predicted in advance of the maturing of concrete circumstances. But knowledge of the laws of social development is of great importance to understand the causes of the great social problems and to know what can be done, and how to ameliorate and end them.

The socioeconomic formation

We live under the capitalist socioeconomic formation. It is an interdependent whole. All aspects help guarantee the existence of all others with respect to the content of their role, even though different aspects are in form different from the same aspects in prior and succeeding socioeconomic formations. In fact, the forms are not exactly the same in any two socioeconomic formations of a capitalist character. Knowing that everything in a socioeconomic formation is interdependent and serves the overall needs of that type of socioeconomic formation—capitalist for example—is the overall framework to understand the formation and its internal laws of development.

Prior to the capitalist socioeconomic formation there first existed the primitive communal socioeconomic formation, before private property and the division into contending classes. Then ancient slave society emerged as the new socioeconomic formation based on the slave-holding class and the labor of slaves. The next socioeconomic formation to emerge was feudalism based on the lords who owned the land and the serfs who were tied to the land and worked it. Capitalism was the next socioeconomic formation to develop, based on the capitalist class that owned the means of production and the working class who owned no means of production and sold their ability to labor to the capitalists. Next to emerge has been the communist formation, called socialism in its first stage.

There have been no other formations and they have developed only in this sequence. This itself strongly refutes any idealist view that denies the development of society according to objectively existing laws eminent in society itself, or sets forward some arbitrary, accidental process.

There are several asterisks to this picture of stages of development of successive socioeconomic formations. For a time Marx and Engels thought there was evidence for another formation in Asia between slave society and feudalism, but they later concluded it was a specific model of feudalism. These developments did not take place in all areas of the world at the same time. Therefore, those entering a more advanced system later could skip to some extent parts of the stages gone through earlier by others or could accomplish the tasks in new ways that did not fully repeat how they were accomplished earlier. Sometimes the transition to the new social system took hundreds of years with more than one episode of slipping back to the old dominant social formation before the new one was lastingly established. We will discuss U.S. chattel slavery later.

Within the socioeconomic formation, what is most decisive in its development?

The mode of production

The law of the central role played by the mode of production in the functioning of a socioeconomic formation was the second great discovery of Marx discussed by Engels at Marx's graveside. What is this law of social development?

The way the necessities of life and the material benefits of society are created is the most decisive aspect of society. It influences all other aspects more than any other aspect influences it or anything else. As discussed, the mode of production consists of two necessary aspects—the forces of production and the relations of production. The forces of production consist of people working with their historically determined level of labor skills, and the means of production including the objects of labor and the means of labor (energy, factories, tools, instruments). Here people are the most important force of production, while instruments of production develop more rapidly than any other aspect of the mode of production.

To be useful, the forces of production require relations of production—how people are related to each other and to the means of production during the process of production. In class society, production relations are property and class relations.

It is a law that the relations of production must correspond to the requirements of the forces of production. That correspondence gives the forces of production, particularly the instruments of production, the possibility to develop at all or more rapidly. At the beginning of a revolution, of a new socioeconomic formation with new relations of production (class or property relations) those relations of production better fit the rapidly changing forces of production (especially instruments of production), so that they are put in conformity with each other. Toward the end of a socioeconomic formation, the relations of production are increasingly in conflict with the forces of production and have become an obstacle to their more rapid advance. That is because the class in power, which dominates the relations of production, resists changes in those relations to better fit the new emerging forces of production. Such resistance takes place because the dominant class stands to lose its wealth and political power if new relations of production displace the old ones.

The contradiction between the advancing forces of production and the relations of production that have come to retard that advance, is the basic contradiction of each class socioeconomic formation and is the deepest cause of the need for a social revolution, a change in the relations of production, the property-class relations so that the old class economic and political domination is replaced with a new leading class. In each socioeconomic formation this basic contradiction has a particular expression.

Under capitalism, the contradiction between the forces of production and the relations of production intensifies as the forces of production become increasingly social and interdependent while property relations consist of private ownership of the means of production by fewer and fewer owners and the private appropriation of what is produced. The basic contradiction that arises from violating the law of the necessity for the relations of production to conform to the needs of the forces of production, and the specific expression of that contradiction under capitalism, give rise to the class struggle and all other major contradictions of capitalism. The resolution to that basic contradiction of capitalism is to replace capitalist relations of production with social relations of production under socialism that correspond to the increasingly social character of the forces of production.

Base and superstructure

The relations of production of a given socioeconomic formation constitutes the base or basis of society on which a superstructure of ideas and organizations covering nearly all other aspects of life takes shape with each new system of relations of production or base. The superstructure serves and defends the existence of that base, of that dominance of a particular class. The superstructure consists of the ideas and organizations in each of the following aspects of life: the state and the political system, legal, philosophical, moral, religious, cultural and aesthetic aspects of society. The dominant ideas and institutions in each of these fields foster the continued dominance of the ruling class in the base. The superstructure also contains rising ideas and institutions in each of these areas that serve the interests of the rising and contending class or classes. When a social revolution takes place as to who holds class (state) power, which is the most important area of the superstructure, dominance in the base changes and which ideas and institutions are dominant in the superstructure also changes. But the superstructure changes more slowly than the relations of production as to which class has become dominant. We will return to some additional qualifications about the relationship of the base and superstructure.

The state

The state is the most important part of the superstructure. It comes into being when private property and classes first develop. It becomes the means of the class owning the means of production and dominating the economy to maintain that position while challenged by the slaves and by those who later become the feudal lords and want the system to be based on serfs who will have some interest in the land and agricultural production. The state is an instrument of power and repression including armed repression. Since its purpose is to maintain power, it is characterized as a political instrument, the epitome and leading instrument of the political system. While Engels developed this theory and historical finding, it was Lenin who developed it further in "State and Revolution" (1916) and other writings. Lenin characterizes the state as an organ of repression and of maintaining power so the dominant class can keep its economic dominance. It consists of the political, military, police and judicial apparatus. No matter what the form of government, whether republic, monarchy, proclaimed dictatorship or liberal bourgeois democracy, all serve to maintain the dominance of the capitalist class in the political and economic systems. Therefore, they are "dictatorships of the bourgeoisie" at the same time that they may be liberal bourgeois republics (a republic involves a governmental structure established by some kind of wide electorate).

In order to be able to replace dominance by the capitalist class and its economy with construction of a socialist economy, a working-class state was necessary. Following Marx and Engels, Lenin called this state the "dictatorship of the proletariat." The working class would have to hold power to accomplish its economic and social aims.

Lenin maintained the dictatorship of the proletariat would be qualitatively more democratic than the most democratic, liberal republic
under the dictatorship of the bourgeoisie. The working class would
share power with its allies and democracy would greatly expand for all
working people under the building and functioning of socialism, as
compared to capitalism. From his experience, Lenin added the concept of an alliance between the proletariat and the poor peasantry and
then in 1921 at the 2nd Congress of the Peoples of the East, added the
nationally oppressed as an ally of the working class, with the working
class leading such an alliance. Marx' and Engels' "dictatorship of the
proletariat" had changed to a state led by the working class in alliance
with the poor peasantry and the nationally oppressed.

A year after "State and Revolution," Lenin further examined developments around monopoly capitalism and concluded that "state
monopoly capitalism" had developed. There was now a merger of the
state with monopoly capitalism. Lenin enlarged his concept of the
state to include not just the organs of repression, but also activities
merging the state with the capitalist economy to help realize capitalist profit. The state could also act to lessen the hardships of the masses of people temporarily and to a limited extent. One consequence
might be lessening working people's dissatisfaction and some partial,
temporary stabilization of capitalism.

This concept of the state is closer to the range of functions of modern governments that combine repression, economic activities and
social welfare functions won by the struggle of the working class and
its allies. Therefore, the phrase in "State and Revolution" about the
need to "smash" the bourgeois state is not likely to have been meant
literally. It was not meant to indicate a need to physically destroy all
parts of the bourgeois state and start from scratch. In Lenin's practice
during the period of the New Economic Policy he made clear that
parts of the old capitalist state and economic structure could be taken
over and used for working-class purposes, thus changing their role
and content while some of their forms remained. And that was done
rather extensively.

The essence of the matter is that under the leadership of the working class a very broad coalition of other class and social forces needs
to be created and to share in rule while constructing the new system.
They need to be able to control the main military and police forces to

make sure the capitalists do not use them to take back power and repress the revolutionary forces. It is even possible for some parts of the state to remain in capitalist hands for a while, without overturning the revolution. Here we are suggesting a possibility about the forms of transition and the means of transition from capitalism to socialist construction which will be discussed.

During the years of Joseph Stalin's dominance as the political and theoretical leader of the progressive forces of the world, a rigidity developed in theory that led to a number of mistakes on the subject of historical materialism and on all other major subjects. No room was given for the superstructure to influence the base, even if to a small extent. Little or no room was given for a new social system to incorporate in its superstructure forms inherited from previous socioeconomic formations and imbue them with a new class meaning in a new socioeconomic formation. Feudalism's male supremacy was used by capitalism to achieve extra profits from the inferior wages women were paid for the same work. While the technocratic interpretation of social development, in which technology determined all social development including relations of production and superstructure, was correctly rejected, there was a mechanical rejection of any influence. Technology could influence changes in form in the superstructure through the class prism of the base. And it could influence the forms of the property relations of the base.

Under the influence of such rigid concepts, the definition of the state returned to that of the forces of repression only and the possibility of a transition without civil war or major violence was eliminated. As late as September 29, 1917—38 days before the November 7 Revolution—Lenin continued to seek a transition without civil war and believed if the Soviets of the Workers, Peasants, the Army and Navy under Menshevik and Bolshevik leadership could unite, they could be so overwhelmingly powerful that the Constituent Assembly would give up pretensions to power peacefully. Shortly after Lenin's death, Stalin wiped out the possibility of peaceful transition by branding it revisionist. Substitution of phrases like "working class" and "working people's power" for "dictatorship of the proletariat" were likewise branded as social democratic and revisionist.

Lenin often argued that though all forms of the bourgeois state represented the dictatorship of the bourgeoisie, its particular form mattered greatly to the working class. Lenin argued the working class should always seek the most democratic form, the most republican form so as to make the workers' struggle easier. He called a lack of concern over the particular form "stupid and self-defeating." As a matter of fact, beginning as early as 1897, continuing to the defeat of the bourgeois democratic revolution of 1905 and in somewhat different form until the victory of the bourgeois democratic revolution in February 1917, Lenin proposed a "democratic revolution" as the first stage of the Russian Revolution. It would replace the czarist autocracy—a repressive regime in the interests of the capitalists with large remainders of feudalism—and expand democracy and democratic rights with a state led by the working class in alliance with the peasantry as a whole. The rising capitalists would be neutralized so that when the democratic revolution was won, it would be much easier to go over to the proletarian, socialist stage of the revolution. In this second stage, the revolution would be led by the working class in alliance with the poor peasantry against the capitalists, neutralizing the middle section of the peasantry. But that path was defeated in 1905 with the victory of the autocracy and did not succeed in February 1917, when the capitalists completed taking power and blocked the working class revolution until November 7.

But the issue of the forms of state rule of the bourgeoisie arose again with the coming of fascism. It was not until the 7th World Congress of the Communist International in 1935 and the Report by its General Secretary, Georgi Dimitrov, that the world Communist movement fully and officially recognized that it did matter to the working class and the democratic masses whether fascism won out in each country and worldwide. The Communists recognized they could and should unite all trends in the working class and the democratic tendency among all other strata, including the capitalists, against fascism in a united front and/or people's front. Fascism was defined as a form of bourgeois state rule—the open terrorist rule of the most reactionary, chauvinistic, militaristic sector of the capitalist class. It arose not out of the strength of capitalism but out of its weakness in the face of the rise of the working class and democratic forces. Something new had arisen in respect to the power of the capitalist class which required a new world strategy to defeat it. That strategy, brought to life in the wartime alliance of the U.S., Britain, France and China and other bourgeois democratic powers with the socialist USSR, was necessary and succeeded in defeating fascism. As late as the 7th World Congress, Stalin held on to old doctrinaire views and he doubted the soundness of Dimitrov's Report, according to some of the U.S. delegates who attended.

Again in 1980 and through the Bush administrations of 2000 and 2004, the Communist Party USA found a political trend within a section of the transnational monopolies for a government with an ultra-right policy. It rules in a conservative, authoritarian manner that severely undermines democratic rights and attacks the interests of the working class and the other democratic sectors. Recognition of this development was necessary to build the broadest possible all-people's front to combat it, limit it and then defeat it. More on this will be discussed under strategy and tactics.

Non-superstructural aspects of society

In studying all aspects of social development, as we have seen, Marx and Engels concluded the mode of production is the most decisive. They then reached their conclusions about the role and interrelationship of the two aspects of the mode of production—the productive forces and the productive relations. Marx and Engels and their successors then came to the conclusions discussed about the base and superstructure, and their nature and role. Then it was necessary to determine whether other important parts of society were part of the base or superstructure. If they were part of neither, how did they fit into social development and the socioeconomic formation?

For a long time there was a tendency to place everything in society automatically into either the base or superstructure. Thus language was placed in the superstructure by Stalin in "Marxism and Linguistics," as though there were one language for the capitalists and a totally different one for the working class. True, there are influences on language of a class nature similar to the superstructure, but while influenced by class, language also has a certain independence and does not simply serve the capitalist class. A similar analysis applies to the laws of the natural and physical sciences. There is not one set of laws for each class, thus putting them in the superstructure. True, the laws of science are used and misused for capitalist profit, war-making, etc. and so there is a close relation with the superstructure of many aspects, but the laws themselves are not superstructural.

Human community: The national question

From the standpoint of history as well as the present, human communities of different kinds—from clan to tribe to nationality to nation—form one of the most important aspects of objective processes of social development. The characteristics of a nation apply equally to different classes—worker, middle strata and capitalist. People belong to the same nation but to different classes.

But the base and superstructure have strong connections with the existence of the different forms of human community and their development. Clans were typical of primitive communal society, prior to private property in the means of production. During slave society tribes and nationalities were typical. Wars of conquest of tribes and nationalities flowed from the base and superstructure of ancient slave society. Under feudalism, the coming together of neighboring peoples with a defined geographical area and language meant the development of nationality. Wars were connected with the interests of the ruling class and the superstructure. There were oppressed nationalities. With capitalism, neighboring nationalities were consolidated into nations and nations became consolidated in a state under a dominant nation. With imperialism, the conquering and oppression of nations and nationalities becomes nearly universal and it reflects both the base and superstructure.

However, those in the same nation have common characteristics as part of that nation even though they are of different classes. In the dominant nations and oppressing nations interests of the capitalist class and the working class are completely incompatible, and a sharp struggle goes on in all aspects of the superstructure. Even here, Marxists are aware that the developed capitalist countries have positive aspects in their history from the progressive forces of each period in their development and that they cannot disregard this history and hope to win over the masses of working people. They must be champions of the best of their history and work to expand that history and tradition.

Marxism defines the nation and distinguishes between oppressor and oppressed nations, nationalities and peoples. A nation possesses a common economy and resulting from that a common territory, common language, common culture and resulting psychological makeup. Earlier the common economy was misunderstood to mean everybody doing the same kind of work rather than a united economy of exchange between different kinds of activity, involving the contending classes. And, that such common economy played the key role in drawing the rest of the characteristics of nationhood into existence, or dispersing them, in the absence of such an economy.

The dominant capitalist nation has aspects that in themselves are not part of the superstructure or base, though there are close ties to those major features of a socioeconomic formation. These include common territory, common language, common culture in its forms (there is the dominant cultural content of the capitalist class and the challenging content of the progressive social forces), and common psychological makeup, which has both non-superstructural forms and class-influenced content. Most if not all of the "common economy" is part of the base or superstructure of the socioeconomic formation.

As for the nationally oppressed nation, nationality, or people, there are parallels to the above but there is more that cuts across class lines in respect to what constitutes an oppressed nation, nationality, or people. The main opponents are the big capitalists of the dominant people. Similarities in interests cut widely across class lines in the struggle to achieve full equality through independence or within the existing state by various means and guarantees. National differences exist with the dominant people and with other oppressed peoples but common class interests with the working class of all peoples also extend across nationality lines.

Lenin fought for oppressed nations to have the democratic right of equality, and therefore the right to statehood if that people as a whole so chose. The Communists of the oppressing people had to support that right. On the other hand the Communists of the oppressed people could advocate achieving full equality either by a separate nation-state or by whatever guarantees they could propose within the same state, according to an estimate as to which would be better for the working class of both nations and their allies. Thus the Russian Communists advocated the right of the Polish people to exercise self-determination by any means up to and including separate nation-statehood from Russia, while the Polish Communists opposed separation and favored full equality within the same state. An oppressed nationality or people, lacking one or more of the qualities of a nation, would not be able to exercise separation successfully and might well simply fall prey to another big power or to the same one in another form. The fight would have to be for advanced autonomy within the existing oppressor state but on the basis of fully equal rights in all respects, except establishing their own state.

The Communists seek unity of the working class of the capitalist powers and the whole of the oppressed people for full equality, and the Communists of the oppressed people seeks leadership of that people by its working class. But that does not always happen, at least for a period of time, and national patriotic forces from the rising bourgeoisie of the oppressed people or even from its armed forces may play the leading role. They may well reflect a nationalism that has its sources in the interests and position of the rising bourgeoisie of the oppressed people. To the extent this nationalism is aimed mainly at achieving independence, it plays a progressive role and to the extent it plays the role of collaboration so that it may be the local boss for the oppressing power, it plays a reactionary role.

While generally the nationalism of an oppressed people plays a progressive role, the highest form of understanding of national relations is that of proletarian internationalism, whether from the standpoint of the oppressor people or the oppressed people. This embodies the concept that the interests of the working class of both peoples are essentially the same. Concerning relations between peoples, proletarian internationalism is superior to all other ideologies, including to an internationalism which is not consistently working class in content. Proletarian internationalism supports the right of all oppressed peoples to self-determination including when one's own capitalists are the source of the oppression. As stated, such self-determination may be expressed by a nation through any form including independent statehood. For a nationality or people, full equality may be expressed through an autonomous region or other means. Among the oppressed people, proletarian internationalism views the working class of the oppressor people not as the source of the oppression but as a potential ally for freedom and equality. Proletarian internationalism also involves a partisan but independent attitude toward countries in which the working class holds power and is constructing socialism.

The oppressed people also has a right to select the means of achieving their freedom, whether by political struggle, plebiscite, various forms of armed struggle or combinations of these. But determining the forms is not to be accomplished by each individual or small group but by the representatives of the majority of the oppressed people. Lenin pointed out that from the standpoint of theory there was a hierarchy of interests when worthy interests conflicted. The interests of social progress and humanity were superior to those of the working class as a whole; the interests of the working class as a whole were superior to those of the nationally oppressed, as important as they are. In practice, however, the choices were not so stark and combinations of interests could be worked out. Thus world public opinion has come to view preventing nuclear war and the use of other weapons of mass destruction to be in the interests of social progress and of humanity. Use of atomic weapons to seek national freedom would be neither just nor successful. The cost would be too great. Nor is the purposeful or careless killing of civilians to achieve national freedom now considered just. It is unjust, and not a permissible method of achieving a just end. It would, therefore, be a violation of proletarian internationalism even though for a just aim.

U.S. nationalities developments

We continue the examination of the place of human community, a non-superstructural aspect of a socioeconomic formation, in terms of relatively recent developments in our own country. Our method of examination is from the standpoint of Marxism, the ideology of the working class. The ethnic or national developments everywhere are quite different but yet have some common features in countries of the capitalist socioeconomic formation. In our country those developments have been extremely complex and are perhaps even more so today.

From the beginning, the 13 colonies fought for their national independence and equality, at first by political means and many forms of political and social struggle and finally by armed struggle and social revolution. At the same time, the Native American peoples were oppressed from the very beginning as they were driven out of their lands and forced to exist in inferior conditions in the colonies and beyond. According to W.E.B. DuBois, African slaves became the first settlers of what became the United States, when their English masters fled the harsh conditions of what is now North Carolina and returned to England. Slavery grew slowly in many of the colonies, including New York, where there were household slaves in the 1790s. But it was not until the cotton gin made cotton a major crop, the base of the economy in the Southern states, that slavery and slaves became a major feature of the national makeup of the country and the ideology of racism grew rapidly to justify it.

At the same time as chattel slavery economy grew rapidly in the Southeast, and as far west as Texas and into the Midwest including Missouri and Kansas, the U.S. bought or acquired by military means a third of the country in the Southwest and West Coast, by war and by theft of one kind or another. This area had belonged to Mexico and contained a substantial population of Mexicans and Native Peoples, who became oppressed peoples in the U.S. They lost much of their lands and rights and became a cheap labor source for the spread and development of U.S. capitalism under the domination of the southern slavocracy of planters, and the beginnings of capitalist manufacturing dominated by people of English origins. In 1815 and later the United States was still also threatened by attempts at British crown restoration.

In the 1840s and 1850s the nationality mix in the country expanded still more. The Irish came fleeing the great famine. Though they hardly looked different than those dominating the country up till then, they were branded an "inferior race." They were assigned hard work at very low wages building the railroads westward and were forced to live in railroad and mining camps in dreadful conditions. Chinese and later other Asians were brought into the country to supply a cheap source of labor on the West Coast to build the railroads eastward and to engage in metal mining—again under subordinate, oppressive conditions only a step higher than slavery, justified by racist rationalizations.

Each new people to come here from Europe at first faced severe forms of discrimination, second-class citizenship and racist justifications that only gradually receded over many years. Only World War II, development of greater mobility to different areas of the country and growth of trade union organization brought significant changes for European ethnic groups. Concerning these sections of the population, it was no longer proper to speak of racist divisions and repression, but rather remnants of old prejudices. Earlier, the bosses in the mass production industries sought to keep the workers apart and fighting each other by placing a different European nationality alone in each department of a factory. This continues today to foster division and "competition" between Black and Latino workers.

Following the defeat of the Revolution of 1848 in Germany and other European countries, many Germans came to New York, Missouri and Kansas, where the more Marxist among them had considerable influence. They played a decisive role in defeating the spread of slavery to these states. They also played a big role in the founding of the labor movement as a national movement. Eventually Germans became the single biggest ethnic group in the U.S., followed by the English. By the end of the 19th century, large numbers of poor workers and farmers from Eastern and Southern Europe and from Scandinavia arrived in different areas of the country. These included Italians, Poles, Hungarians, Jews, Swedes, Finns, etc. These ethnic groups went through the general process described earlier. Because of a number of factors such as religious sources of anti-Semitism, the rise of fascism and the holocaust of World War II, Jews experienced various forms of special oppression longer.

While the Civil War realigned the country and ended slavery, it did not end the oppression of African Americans nor end racism. As Marx pointed out, the slave-owning system of plantation agriculture created a rapid accumulation of capital and enabled the faster development of industrial capitalism in the U.S., so that by the time of World War I the U.S. was a contender for the strongest capitalist power in the world. The democratic revolution in the South was cut short by the Hayes-Tilden Compromise of 1876 and even reversed to a considerable extent. The result was that most of the former slaves became tenant farmers and sharecroppers under a semi-feudal system. The former slaves experienced extreme repression in the Jim Crow system of segregation that took hold. This included legal and illegal lynchings and other forms of severe repression and second-class existence until the Civil Rights Revolution of the 1960s (the Second Stage of the Democratic Revolution in the South begun in the Civil War).

With the U.S. entering its imperialist stage at the end of the 1800s and the first major imperialist war—that of the U.S. against Spain, the Philippines, and Cuba—the U.S. began to see an influx of people from the Philippines, Cuba, Puerto Rico, the Dominican Republic and other Central American and Caribbean areas. Being of a darker color, often with Spanish as their first language, coming from poorer countries

where they were poor farmers and were able to get very little education, and having arrived in the U.S. later than some of the European
peoples, the pattern of oppression, racism and second-class status was
not defeated so easily and their merger with other peoples did not take
place so smoothly. When they first arrived they often settled next to or
even among earlier Spanish speakers in areas where Latin cultures
existed. In the case of Puerto Rico, it became and still is a colony.
Puerto Ricans in New York, other East Coast areas and the Midwest
number as many as those remaining in Puerto Rico. They are U.S. citizens but are one of the poorest national groups both on the island and
in the U.S.

After World War I and again after World War II large numbers of
African Americans migrated from the rural and urban South to the
industrial centers of the North to find work in the mass production
industries. African Americans became a majority in cities in the Mid-
Atlantic, Northeast and Midwest, or made up at least a quarter of the
population, in Washington, D.C.; Baltimore; Philadelphia, New York,
New Haven and Hartford, Conn.; Buffalo, Pittsburgh, Cleveland;
Detroit; Gary, Ind.; Chicago, St. Louis, Milwaukee, Houston,
Oakland, Calif.; San Francisco and Los Angeles. The system of discrimination and oppression of African Americans remains a central
feature of U.S. life and is a particular source of the strength of the
ultra-right and other sections of big capital. With capitalist globalization and the decline of mass industrial production in the cities, and the
growth of robber-baron developers in these cities driving up housing
and other costs, there has been some significant outflow of African
Americans and other older nationally oppressed groups from some of
the cities and a decline of their living standards.

Since World War II many Arab and other Muslim peoples have
migrated to the U.S., settling especially in New York, Los Angeles,
Detroit and Chicago. South Asians have come to New York and other
big cities. Large numbers of Afro-Caribbean people have migrated to
Brooklyn, N.Y. and nearby areas, and Latinos have come to the New
York City area from Central America and Caribbean islands. This
migration reflects the worldwide trend of people from poorer countries moving to the most developed, richer countries in search of a better life. They are then compelled to supply unskilled labor especially
in construction, agriculture, the food industry, health care, child care

and similar industries. Together with large numbers of new immigrants from Mexico, and immigrants from China and other Eastern and South Asian nations, they have joined the nationally and racially oppressed in our country with fewer rights, lower incomes and living standards. Since the end of socialism in Eastern Europe, there has been an influx of Russians, Poles and others. Undocumented immigrants especially suffer every form of oppression including vicious raids by immigration authorities, resulting in separation of families through large-scale deportations.

As a result of all these developments, a complex ethnic-nationality process is taking place. On the one hand all peoples in the U.S. are being drawn into a single U.S. nation with a common economy and territory, increasingly English speaking, though Spanish is a secondary and even a primary language in some areas. Common cultural and psychological features are developing alongside features that reflect the countries of origin. The mass media and means of communication and the highly integrated economy continue to push these developments forward overall. And yet special oppression of many of these peoples simultaneously draws them together of necessity and as a source of strength to resist the oppression. Mexicans living in Los Angeles, Texas, Chicago and New York are drawn into relations with the surrounding peoples, the people of the whole country and with Mexicans in all these locations. Other Latinos who come to live within or near the general Mexican American population have sources of identity both with people of their country of origin where they live and across the country, and with Mexicans around them and all Latinos across the country.

Similar processes are taking place among people from East Asia, with Chinese people emerging as the largest segment. Afro-Caribbeans are relating to one another across countries of origin and with African Americans and newly arrived Africans. In this mix African Americans are the pivot, though among Afro-Caribbeans themselves, Jamaicans play a central role. Among the nationally and racially oppressed, at times and on particular issues, the tendency predominates to identify with the whole U.S. nation. But at other moments and on other issues, the tendency predominates to identify with a regional set of peoples, or with one specific homeland.

With the passage of time the long-term tendency is to identify more with the general and less with the specific. But continued special national and racial oppression tends to slow down this process and even reverse it at times. It is necessary for the progressive forces of all national backgrounds to defend the rights of the nationally and racially oppressed to maintain their special identity as this is a necessary weapon in the fight for full equality until it is actually achieved. The drawing together of people into a single U.S. nation under capitalism is a combination of the pressure of assimilation of oppressed peoples and amalgamation of cultures of peoples into something new that continues the best of each. But under capitalism this can only happen in a limited and distorted way.

Most of the nationally and racially oppressed peoples are heavily working class. The process of the growth of the U.S. working class involves the gradual drawing together of all of its national group components into one unified class.

Full real equality cannot be lastingly achieved while capitalism exists as the capitalists gain from the existence of national and racial oppression and continually want to reintroduce it even where it is defeated. They gain extra surplus value and profit when wages are lower for work of comparable worth. They may actually be able to pay the nationally oppressed worker below the value of his or her labor power and thus reap even more surplus value. And by weakening and dividing the workers, the capitalist may be able not only to pay the nationally oppressed worker below the value of his or her labor power but also to pay the white worker below the value of his or her own labor power, increasing surplus value still more. Thus only when capitalism is ended is it possible to introduce broad compensatory programs so the nationally oppressed can catch up and achieve full equality. Then with the passage of some time, amalgamation of different peoples into one can occur, taking the best from the accomplishments of each, and one socialist people as a whole can emerge, as Lenin predicted. This is not likely to be achieved in the beginning of socialism as it will take some time to develop.

The class struggle

Once we have examined the various major aspects of a socioeconomic formation and their interrelationships that have existed over history and are present today, the question is—what is key in determining their movement and the direction of that movement? In "The Manifesto," Marx and Engels argued that the class struggle was the motor of history in all class-divided societies. According to Marxism, classes are large groups of people defined by their conflicting relationships to the means of production in the process of production. There is a dominant class which owns the means of production of that socioeconomic formation and dominates the state.

There is also the mass of producers, of those who labor who are related in different ways to the predominant forces of production of each formation.

For further discussion of the class struggle and the working class see Chapter 2, **Defining the Working Class and Productive Work**, and the first section of this chapter.

The class struggle severely weakens the ruling class and opens the door for a new ruling class to emerge based on the changes in the forces of production requiring a new system of relations of production.

But in the case of capitalism, the system gives rise to the necessary struggle by the capitalists constantly to extract more surplus value and profit from the working class. It gives rise to the struggle by the working class initially to improve its living standards by trying to keep more of the new value it creates, to reduce the surplus value, to increasingly oppose all the other evils of capitalism that grow on this base and eventually to end the system entirely. But in this case the working class seeks to and does replace the capitalist class as the ruling class and to replace capitalism with socialism. The class struggle between the working class and the capitalist class is inherent in capitalism and cannot be halted, no matter what the capitalists do, whether ideologically trying to convince the working class their interests are the same, or repression against trade unions and other workers' organizations. The capitalists must continually try to extract more surplus value, and the workers as a class have no way to hold on to their living conditions—let alone improve them—but to struggle in a variety of ways against the capitalist class.

Underlying the class struggle is the growing contradiction between the increasingly social, interdependent forces of production and the increasingly narrowly-based relations of production under private capitalist ownership of the means of production and distribution. As a result, the basic law of capitalism increasingly comes into play—the necessity for a fundamental change in the relations of production so that they also become social in nature, socially owned. This basic contradiction gives rise to the class struggle and other contradictions of capitalism.

Initially, the class struggle is spontaneous; individual or small groups of workers demanding higher wages, less speed-up, greater safety measures on the job, shorter hours. They then begin to combine to withhold their labor if they do not win their demands—undertaking strikes, slowdowns and other forms of struggle. They combine permanently into trade unions, better to fight for these things and to protect themselves from retaliation by the boss, including firing and other punishment for forming unions. At this stage the class struggle is fought on the basis of the development of trade union consciousness. Workers then begin to realize legislation and election of particular people can help them achieve their needs, including unemployment and workmen's compensation, occupational safety protections, even health protection. They come to recognize the need for demands not directly connected with their employment, that can be won in the legislative and electoral arenas to make life easier and better. Among these are public education through college, day care, public subsidy and truly affordable, decent public housing.

Workers develop consciousness that the fight for peace is in the interests of workers, as workers and their children do the fighting, war diverts their tax money into harmful uses and achieves nothing for the workers but is rather in the interests of the capitalists. The workers come to understand their class interest includes the need for full equality across all racial and nationality lines, across gender, immigration status, and lines of sexual preference. They learn that the fight for expansion of democracy and against limitation of democratic rights is in the interests of the workers and the class struggle. The working class especially needs the right to organize and strike in an unfettered way. The working class needs a sustainable environment and economy and must struggle against the profiteers of capitalism on this and all other issues.

The arenas and the forms of the class struggle expand. They start from the point of production directly over the division of the new value the workers create but expand to all the other issues discussed.

The struggles take place in the economic arena at the point of production and also the legislative arena that can often influence the division of the new value created. They develop in the political arena to pass legislation favorable to the working class, and to elect people friendly to labor. Then struggles develop to elect representatives of the working class themselves and to develop parties led by labor. These struggles must also be fought in the ideological arena, for ideas favorable to the interests of the working class and against ideas that are anti-labor or preach class collaboration on the basis of the domination of capitalist class interests. In our country racism is the most prevalent and dangerous of the ruling class' ideological weapons. Racism is a form of class collaboration. Anti-communism has also been a potent weapon of the capitalist class in the ideological arena. Male supremacy, anti-immigrant, and anti-LGBT ideology are also ideological aspects of the class struggle.

It is necessary first to develop trade union consciousness and then increasingly complete class consciousness so that the working class becomes not just a class unto itself but a class that sees and acts for itself as opposed to the capitalist class because it understands the class meaning of developments on all social issues. Within this developed class consciousness it is necessary that socialist consciousness and the most consistent ideology of the working class, Marxism, emerges as a current among the working class. As we shall see, this can only take place as a significant current among the working class and all the oppressed and exploited and working people in and through a Communist Party.

There is a never-ending development of the forms and combinations of forms of the class struggle. These include slowdown, work to rule, brief work stoppages, strikes, all kinds of legislative and electoral activities, demonstrations, mass rallies, general strikes, completely peaceful revolutions involving many of these mass forms of action and representing a majority of the people, use of some or a lot of military force, from a military show of force to actual combat, guerrilla style or with major combat units or all kinds of combinations of some or all of these.

A revolution can come about in a day or an extended period of time or in stages separated by periods of relative quietude. It can involve changing who holds power in each sector of the government all at once or by separate steps, a department at a time, with power shifting gradually from the capitalist class holding it to the working class. There can be a dual power for a time as there was in Russia between the Soviets and the Constituent Assembly. The leaders of the working-class movement will certainly take into account the existence of the weaponry now in the hands of the capitalist class, including nuclear weapons, and will do everything to achieve a peaceful road for the working people to complete a revolution in which capitalist political power is ended and the means of production are gradually transferred from the hands of capitalists to a variety of forms of social ownership on the decision of the democratic representatives of the working class. From the whole course of world and U.S. development, there are good grounds to believe a transition can be accomplished without significant military action. The most crucial aspect is assembling the largest majority possible of the working class, its allies and all the working people, which can be very overwhelming, to guarantee success.

The logical outcome of the working class' position under capitalism and of its struggle to advance its interests is a socialist revolution to replace capitalism with a working class-led state and society. That requires the working class to lead a vast assemblage of allies starting with the nationally oppressed, women and youth and including all working people. That is both possible and necessary.

The class struggle and the democratic struggle

The class struggle moves all progressive struggles and social development forward step by step until the change takes place in who holds power and the process begins to change, over time or relatively rapidly, the ownership of the means of production and distribution from private capitalist, to forms of social ownership on the road to socialism and then to full communist society. That is why Marx and Engels found the class struggle to be the motive force of history. It is through its existence that the qualitative change is made from one socioeconomic formation to another. The class struggle under capitalism also takes place in conjunction with the democratic struggle. All struggles by the working class for its interests against the capitalist class are directly a part of the class struggle and the ultimate aim of that struggle is power and replacing the capitalist class.

The democratic struggle is a struggle in which all class and social forces who have an interest can be won to participate. It takes place over all the issues just discussed. Its aim is to widen the arena for struggle on all these issues and to create conditions for the class struggle to be able to fight and win. Such democratic space can be enlarged by quantitative steps of the everyday struggle by some or all of the democratic forces—the working class, the core forces, all working people. It can also involve qualitative changes in the relationship of forces, such as the defeat of a particularly reactionary section of the transnational monopolies in governmental power. Previously it involved the defeat of the fascist danger in the U.S. in the 1930s and fascism internationally by 1945.

The democratic struggle advances the class struggle by weakening the monopoly capitalist class and strengthening the working class. It opens up the possibility for the victory of the class struggle to end capitalism. By the same token the class struggle strengthens and advances the democratic struggle by bringing the working class into all democratic struggles, increasingly in a leading role and weakening the section of capital being attacked for the purpose of democratic advance. Thus the class struggle and the democratic struggle are closely intertwined and mutually reinforcing, yet not identical.

4 Socialism and Communism

❖ Marx and Engels establish socialism theoretically
❖ Lenin's contribution, before the revolution, to the theory of socialist revolution
❖ Developing socialism under Lenin's leadership
❖ U.S. socialism
❖ The Chinese revolution
❖ The Vietnamese revolution
❖ The Cuban revolution
❖ Venezuela and the Latin American wave to the left
❖ Lessons from building socialism under Stalin's leadership
❖ Lessons from the Soviet experience, 1953 until its demise

Once one concludes that capitalism is incompatible with the interests of the working class and all working people, that it increasingly threatens the very existence of humanity, and that it cannot be patched up, then the issue is whether there is an alternative to capitalism and whether that alternative is socialism. In their studies of the development of society, of historical materialism, Marx and Engels concluded that capitalism needed to be and would be replaced by nothing other than socialism. They concluded socialism would make it possible to solve most of the burning problems facing the working class, all working people, and humanity as a whole.

In this chapter we shall examine the theoretical conclusions of Marx and Engels with regard to socialism and how they developed them. We will then examine Lenin's further development of these conclusions before and after the Russian Revolution: his experience in leading the early construction of socialism. Then in the light of the contributions of Marx, Engels and Lenin about socialism, we will discuss socialism in the U.S. based on our history and conditions. We will then look at some of the experience of socialist construction now taking place in the world—in China, Vietnam, Cuba and the new wave toward socialism in Venezuela and elsewhere in Latin America. Finally, we will examine what we can learn from the experience of the Soviet Union after Lenin, until its demise.

Marx and Engels establish socialism theoretically

Marx and Engels concluded from their historical and theoretical studies that each succeeding class-divided society gave rise to contradictions and class struggle that could only be resolved by replacement of the existing socioeconomic system by a new one that resolved the basic contradiction of the previous one. The conditions requiring the new socioeconomic system and making it possible were being built up while the previous system continued to be dominant. We discussed this process in terms of new forces of production coming increasingly into conflict with the existing relations of production, or class, property relations. For the forces of production, especially its instruments to advance fully, the retarding class or property relations had to be changed to conform.

With capitalism, the contradiction was between the increasingly social, interdependent forces of production coming more and more into conflict with the capitalist relations of production in which ownership of the means of production and distribution were in fewer and fewer hands. The capitalists wanted no change in the relations of production that would undermine their power and ownership. Because the capitalist system was based on extracting surplus value from the unpaid labor of the working class, the working class was compelled to struggle against the capitalist class. From these processes inherent in capitalism, Marx and Engels concluded the working class would lead a revolution which would end capitalist ownership of the means of production and distribution and replace it with "public ownership," "social ownership," or as they first termed it in "The Communist Manifesto," "nationalized property" owned by the working class in the form of the dictatorship of the proletariat. This would overcome the basic contradiction of capitalism and put the relations of production in harmony with the forces of production. It would replace production for the purpose of maximizing private profit and property with production for social use, to better the lives of the vast majority of the people.

Marx and Engels had studied the utopian socialists—Henri de Saint-Simon, Charles Fourier, Robert Owen. They too had observed all the immense social injustices of their times. But the utopians did not understand the capitalist economy, the extraction of surplus value, the resulting class struggle and the position and role of the working class, nor did they understand historical materialism and the laws requiring that one social system replace another. They looked for schemes and experimental colonies to end the ills of capitalism and achieve justice and equality. Marx and Engels gave a scientific meaning to the concepts of equality and justice.

In "The Manifesto," the point was made that the first step in the revolution needed to be the working class taking state power. That concept is discussed in the previous chapter in relation to the state. Marx and Engels understood as early as 1848 that transforming capitalist property (means of production) into "nationalized property of the working class state" was not a single act but would take time. Another cardinal task would be to increase production as rapidly as possible. As capitalist property was swept away so would classes disappear, as would the need for the political power of a state to impose the will of the dominant class. Production would be placed in the hands of a vast "free association" of the people. In this classless, stateless association the "free development of each is the condition for the free development of all."

By the time of Marx's "Critique of the Gotha Programme" in 1875 and the last version of Engels' "Socialism: Utopian and Scientific," they had added to and developed these conclusions. They did not speak of "nationalized" property at all but spoke of "public property" and "socialized property." They foresaw an extended period of time of socialism before classes and the state would "wither away." During what came to be called the "socialist phase" of the "communist socioeconomic formation," they saw work being remunerated on the basis of the quantity and quality of the work performed. During the "communist phase" of the system, payment would be on the principle of "from each according to his (her) ability, to each according to his (her) need." They made clear "each according to need" assumed society had reached the point where production was so plentiful that it could be the basis of payment for work. It would also be a period in which the distinctions between physical and mental labor and between town and country would be gradually eliminated.

Lenin's contribution, before the revolution,
to the theory of socialist revolution

Building on Marx and Engels, in 1902-03 Lenin developed the theory of the party of the new type, concluding that without the building of a Communist Party and its playing the leading role among the working class and other strata it would not be possible to win state power to build socialism. We will discuss this theory of the Communist Party and later developments in the last chapter.

As discussed under "The State" in the last chapter, Lenin developed the concept of the dictatorship of the proletariat to include the idea that this could be expressed through a working-class-led coalition of those class and social forces whose interests favored the change in state power and were won to play that role. In Russia this meant the poor peasantry, and Lenin later added the nationally oppressed.

Another major question was whether the change in power could come about only by force, civil war or large-scale violence. Marx and Engels had examined this question several times. At one time they believed such a transition to the dictatorship of the proletariat could be accomplished only by major armed struggle. But then they found a period in which the U.S. and Britain had minimal armed forces and they saw these as exceptional situations that permitted a "peaceful transition" with lots of mass struggle but no major violence. When the situation changed and both countries greatly enlarged their armed forces, Marx and Engels concluded such a possibility no longer existed.

The issue of whether the transition to the dictatorship of the proletariat could be accomplished without civil war or significant violence was also discussed in connection with the question of where the proletarian revolution would first break out. It was generally thought it would happen in the most developed capitalist countries—Great Britain, Germany, France. But at one point, Marx and Engels suggested it might first occur in Russia because of the severe repression and weak, backward state.

Lenin, in his "April Theses" of 1917, said a peaceful transition without civil war was desirable from the standpoint of the working class and saw a moment in the balance of forces in Russia to make that possible. But after Bloody Friday, July 2, when the Constituent Assembly bourgeois government of Kerensky made a bloody assault on the Soviets, Lenin concluded it would not be possible and began planning an armed overthrow. But again in September, as discussed in the previous chapter, Lenin saw a change in the balance of forces.

He was still seeking a peaceful transition. Lenin wrote that if all of the Soviets united, the capitalist government would have no chance of winning a military conflict and might recognize that and surrender. (Lenin, V.I., "The Russian Revolution and Civil War," Sept. 29, 1917, CW Vol. 26, pp. 36-37.) But while the Soviets achieved a high level of unity, it was not complete and an armed insurrection was necessary. No major armed struggle took place immediately following that event of November 7. The Civil War grew out of the armed intervention of the 14 imperialist powers in 1918 and 1919.

Another major issue on the eve of the revolution was whether a revolution could be successful in a single country. Lenin argued it could be done due to the internal and worldwide balance of forces, including divisions in the ranks of imperialism. The Mensheviks and Leon Trotsky (who had been a Menshevik until joining Lenin's Bolshevik Party in 1915) argued it would not be possible. Trotsky misinterpreted Marx's concept of "permanent revolution" to mean that if the Bolsheviks won in Russia they should proceed militarily and bring socialism to neighboring countries until a world revolution occurred. Marx meant that once there was a revolutionary process somewhere in a developed country, the process would begin to extend itself elsewhere by force of example and could not be stopped from continually spreading. In that sense it would become permanent. Marx' discussion in different periods of where the socialist revolution might first occur, implied that there could be some time between the revolution in the first country to rebel and those in succeeding countries.

The Mensheviks also argued Russia was too backward economically and socially to support a revolution to socialism. It would have to occur in a more developed country and therefore, no revolution should be attempted there. Lenin responded with evidence that Russia was basically capitalist and that its backwardness meant it was the weakest big power in Europe, the weakest link in the chain of imperialism, that it could be overthrown. Trotsky and others maintained socialism could not be built in a single country and for that and other reasons the revolution would have to be exported to other countries to succeed.

Lenin argued the revolution could not be exported to other countries and peoples. That would violate the principles of the national question, the right to self-determination as to social system.

Attempting to impose socialism on any other people would endanger the success of the revolution in Russia. Lenin at first expected other countries to soon follow Russia's lead and take the path of revolution—Germany and Hungary in particular.

But those revolutions were drowned in blood. The invasion of Russia by 14 capitalist powers including the U.S. was followed by a civil war in which imperialist countries supported the counterrevolutionary White Army and other regional armies. At that time, Lenin maintained the position that a single country, Russia, could continue to exist and develop as a socialist country for a long period until other countries broke away from capitalism.

Reading the whole of Marx, Engels and Lenin's works in their proper time sequence, we are struck by how they constantly developed Marxism, taking into account all major new developments, yet held to its basic propositions, its class outlook and its methodology. On more than one occasion each of them looked back and corrected earlier predictions and estimates. They particularly took note of a subjective tendency to underestimate difficulties ahead and overestimate the speed of positive developments. We can say now that the Marxists misestimated the particularities of the situation of each country, each country's stage of development, and complications in each country that would make the path to socialism and the form of socialism considerably different everywhere. With the passage of time, capitalism also undergoes considerable changes, especially now with globalization. As long as capitalism remains dominant in the world, its new developments have a big impact on how working class power is won in any particular country and what socialism looks like in each country. One conclusion from this is that each country taking the socialist road needs to study all prior experience, but must still approach building socialism in its own country as though it is a new experience. There is no path that is easy, that is all successes, without difficulties, setbacks and mistakes, that is not a novel experiment in the historic advance of humankind.

Developing socialism under Lenin's leadership

The overriding slogan of the Russian Revolution was "Peace, Bread and Land." The Communists presented this as the aim and a revolution to construct socialism as the necessary means to achieve it.

Bread epitomized what the working class and other starving masses of Russia needed. Land was what the poor peasants needed. And
peace was necessary for national salvation and to be able to achieve
the other two demands.

The great difficulties Russia faced in the first years after the revolution were due to the economic and social devastation of World War
I, the backwardness of czarist Russia, the invasion of the imperialist
powers and then the civil war. Lenin sought ways to consolidate mass
support and ease the situation as quickly as possible. These included
his support for the Treaty of Brest-Litovsk to take Russia out of the
war with Germany. This involved a compromise in which Poland and
other areas would be given up. At first Lenin was in a minority in supporting it. Trotsky, the war minister, with his concept of permanent
revolution and leftist tendency already in evidence, was in the majority. But Lenin convinced the party and government leadership that to
win the support of the soldiers as a whole and the peasants from
whom the army came, peace was needed right away. If not, the revolution as a whole faced the real possibility of defeat.

The economy in this first period was characterized as "war communism." The needs of the revolutionary military forces and key sectors
of the economy were commandeered, including food from the peasants and various requirements from the capitalists. This caused hostil-
ity from forces the revolution needed as allies or passive sympathiz-
ers, and sectors of the economy that still needed to function under capitalist methods.

At the same time, the active supporters of the revolution were full
of initiative and enthusiasm to build a better life in every area. All
kinds of self-help social services developed to aid those most in trouble, including the camps of Anton Makarenko for troubled youth and
the educational efforts of Nadezhda Krupskaya and Mikhail Kalinin.
Cultural life in all areas began to flourish and was full of experimen-
tation especially as the 1920s began. Isadora Duncan and many others
from around the world were drawn to Russia to participate. Exciting
new works were produced by writers and composers such as Gorky,
Sholokhov, Mayakovsky, Shostakovich and Prokofiev. No heavy hand
limited these experiments. As the state could, it extended resources to
support such activities, as well as people's organizations in the arts.

The pogroms and all other forms of social oppression of minority peoples were ended. Formal equality of peoples was proclaimed by law right away and Lenin proclaimed the concept that oppressed peoples needed compensatory measures to gain equality in conditions of living, culture and self-rule. Despite the meager material resources, first steps in this direction were taken, whether it was establishing a local or regional Soviet of oppressed people or developing a written alphabet for peoples lacking it. Literacy programs were a big item.

But in 1921 Lenin and his supporters recognized the need to end war communism in the economy and replace it with the New Economic Policy (NEP). Stalin, who reluctantly supported the NEP, said in closing it down soon after Lenin's death, that it had been a necessary retreat but the retreat was over. The purpose of the NEP was not to retreat but to advance production of industrial and agricultural commodities as rapidly as possible. To do that, market mechanisms were used in much of the economy. Some industries were nationalized or owned at the republic level or by a city and some producers' cooperatives entered the market. Much of agriculture including the middle peasant holdings remained private, but sold their products on the market under various regulations.

Capitalist industrial and other enterprises were allowed in many fields and sometimes there was mixed private and state ownership. Foreign capitalist concessions were allowed in some fields under regulation. Lenin argued that the working class and communist managers needed to learn alongside the capitalists to be able to take over and do a good job. Maximizing production as quickly as possible was crucial to winning the support of the peasant masses and many others for the revolution. To those who worried about restoration of capitalism, Lenin replied that so long as the working class held state power under the leadership of the Communist Party, restoration would not be permitted. He characterized these capitalist-led enterprises as a state capitalist sector.

In two of the last five articles of his life, considered his last testament, Lenin argued that what should follow the NEP should be the dominance of producers' cooperatives in agriculture, with some also in other sectors of the economy. The peasants should be persuaded by bonuses to enter these cooperatives. The land and the factories should be state-owned.

As to political structure and democracy, Lenin pushed for a federal state based on Soviets, including Soviets governing each republic and autonomous republic. A truly federated state was not accomplished fully before Lenin left the scene. Stalin moved back from it and built a unitary state, still defined as "federated," which in life often violated national rights.

Lenin sought a multi-party state. The government at first included not only the Bolshevik Party but also the Left Socialist Revolutionary Party. It was only after that party attempted a coup and attempted to assassinate Lenin that Russia became a one-party state.

At the end of his life Lenin expressed concern that there remained a long way to go so that the country was in fact governed by the working class as a whole and all working people. Lenin acknowledged that it was still governed by the Communist Party and its active supporters. He said what took place was unavoidable. It would take time but the objective remained to involve the whole working class and its allies in actual governing. He called for a fight against bureaucratic tendencies and proposed next steps to increase democratic input.

With this background in the theory of socialism as presented by Marx, Engels and Lenin, and Lenin's practice of it until 1924, let us consider socialism in the context of the United States.

U.S. socialism

What will be the starting point to build socialism in the U.S.? How can we be confident it will solve the ills of capitalism and fulfill its great promise? Socialism will start out with a great majoritarian coalition of the popular democratic forces determining to overcome social problems by radically curbing the economic, political and ideological power of the transnational monopolies. Having achieved some victories, this broad working class led coalition will conclude at some point it is necessary to replace capitalism as a whole with socialism to eliminate the most pressing social ills it then confronts, whether another economic crisis, extremes of poverty and wealth, severe limitations on democratic rights, another war, the sharpening of the environmental crisis.

The issue may then be how to advance from a people's anti-monopoly government significantly limiting the power of the monopolies to a government that aims to construct socialism by replacing monopoly capital ownership of the commanding heights of the economy with a ic political system that will uphold socialist construction.

To win power in our country in order to construct socialism, it will be necessary to build on the broad anti-monopoly coalition, creating an even vaster coalition of class and social forces led by the working class. This will have to be done in close alliance with all the core forces of U.S. progressive advance—the working class, the nationally and racially oppressed, women and youth—together with working people as a whole. They will constitute the overwhelming majority of the people of our country.

The Communist Party for years assumed that as the struggle advanced toward more radical goals, the alliance would narrow. But as monopolies have become dominant under capitalism, and have been transformed into transnational monopolies, experience has shown there is less and less opportunity for the middle strata to become full-fledged capitalists or to consistently improve their lives in other ways. Illusions about such possibilities are dying away not only among the middle strata but also among those sections of the working class who are not won early-on to understand that their class interests lie in replacing capitalism with socialism.

Thus the tendency is for the opposition to capitalism to grow wider and wider. That is very important because the necessity has become so much greater for a working-class alliance of all these class and social forces to win power in a way that makes the transition free of any serious armed struggle. With the existence of weapons of mass destruction and highly destructive conventional weapons, the urgency of a "peaceful transition" has become much greater. Before masses will be willing to do all that is necessary in and out of the electoral arena to win power and establish a government committed to construct socialism, they will want every possible assurance that it can be accomplished without significant military action. And as Lenin pointed out in September 1917 (Lenin, V.I., "The Russian Revolution and Civil War," Sept. 29, 1917, CW Vol. 26, pp. 36-37) in the first place that depends on how overwhelming the mass support for working class-led power is.

The CPUSA's program, "The Road to Socialism USA," projects that the U.S. form of working-class power (dictatorship of the proletariat) will be led by the working class and include an alliance of all the core forces and working people in a multi-party government. This is both because of U.S. history and culture and because such a wide array of class and social forces will certainly express themselves through a variety of parties for some time before they can gradually draw together in fewer or even one party. It is also possible that the present pattern of two major parties—but not the present two parties in content—will continue. The class leadership and role of parties will have to change to fit the needs of constructing a socialist society.

Socialism will be constructed on the basis of expanding the democratic rights achieved during our history, starting with the Declaration of Independence and the Constitution, especially the Bill of Rights. If they have not already been won, this will include such things as the right to a job and living wage; the right to live in peace; the right to live completely free of racism and of oppression of women, with full rights for the LGBT community; the right to a free, quality education through college; the right to health care; the right to affordable housing; the right to live in an environment and economy that are sustainable; abolition of the death penalty. While other countries have been unable to enact all such measures because of the insufficient economic base with which they started to construct socialism, that will not be our case. We will build on the democratic rights that have been won by progressive struggle. And we will take strong steps to overcome the legacy of what is negative in our history such as racism and male supremacy. This will require affirmative action, compensatory treatment and special, all-sided programs with major funding to provide first-class living conditions in all respects for historically nationally and racially oppressed peoples.

Right from the beginning of working people's power, it will be necessary to draw the working people as a whole into forms of participation in making all the major decisions of the government and of the economy so the decisions can be the best possible, so the people as a whole feel invested in their success and so they will be the active builders of the new society. Such involvement is an immensely crucial condition for success from the earliest stages.

In winning working-class-led power and setting out to construct socialism, our people will be able to draw on the theory and practice of Marxism, starting with Marx, Engels and Lenin. We will be able to draw on the lessons of Lenin's leadership of the winning of power and early construction of the world's first working-class state toward socialism. We will be able to draw on all the successes and mistakes in many countries of the world. Undoubtedly many more countries will be constructing socialism when we take that path.

We will also be able to draw on our country's entire history. We can learn from its reactionary past what to fight and how. Above all, we can build on the democratic and progressive movements, moods, ideas and activities of the masses of working people who brought us to the brink of winning power and constructing a U.S. socialism.

Based on what the leaders and masses of working people constructing socialism will have to draw on, including considerably more favorable objective conditions and traditions than the first builders of socialism had, it is reasonable to expect they will avoid the big mistakes, and even crimes against socialism, of earlier efforts. In building a new society, we undoubtedly will experience big successes along the way. But since every new country taking the path of socialism undertakes an experiment in unique conditions, we will also make some mistakes of our own.

According to the CPUSA's program, democratic rights in our country must include the right of the majority to decide what social system they want. We demand that going forward to socialism. Should the socialist government make many unforeseen mistakes and lose the confidence of the people, they may replace it with another government pledged to socialism. If the mistakes are serious enough, the result may even be a referendum on socialism or not. The Communist Party will insist on a level playing field, including that what remains of capitalist wealth may not be used to determine the outcome. The Communist Party will abide by the results of such a referendum and start over again rebuilding mass support and a new take on how to govern and keep popular support. The program says that like every other government in the world, a Communist-led government will not allow the overthrow of the government and the system by armed force, a coup, or other undemocratic or unconstitutional means.

If private ownership of the media by the transnational monopolies has not already been ended, a Communist-led government will enact that and divide the media among the allied political parties and all kinds of popular movements and organizations, starting with the labor movement, guaranteeing a variety of opinions including those of opponents of the government.

In order to sustain such measures, the economy will have to continue at a high level and even increase rapidly its output of a variety of products, services and information. To accomplish this the following measures will be necessary in guiding the economy:

• Investing the workers with a high level of ownership and control over the running of the production and distribution facilities, including making decisions about wages, conditions, promotions, what is produced and how to economize on production inputs, etc.

• Eliminating the huge differences in income under capitalism so that everyone is paid according to the value of the work they perform while contributing according to their ability. This requires eliminating unearned forms of income over a period of time.

• Beginning with a variety of forms of social ownership and limited private ownership. This may include cooperatives; public ownership at the city, state and national level; mixed forms of ownership and private ownership where that will help the building of socialism.

• Use of market mechanisms under regulation and national, state and city plans, to promote competition in price, quantity, quality, variety and costs and efficiency of production.

When the U.S. takes the path of socialism, more countries will already have taken that path and we will be able to benefit from and contribute to a world socialist division of labor. Since our country is the main fomenter of imperialist aggression and supplies arms to the rest of the world, it is likely that when we take the road to socialism, it can be a road free of war and the threat of war. The road to socialism can be free of the serious threat of outside intervention to restore capitalism. Most of the cost of the military can be permanently eliminated.

Now let us look at examples of present-day socialism to see how they are doing, what they can build on from the past, what they have learned to avoid, and what their experience might mean for U.S. socialism.

The Chinese revolution

Lenin called the American, French and Russian Revolutions the three greatest revolutions in history as they made the most far-reaching changes. If he had lived until 1949, he would surely have added the Chinese Revolution to that list. There was the great ancient history and culture and the size and poverty of the population. For a hundred years the imperialist powers had sought to rob China and dismember it. From the time Japanese imperialism invaded Manchuria in 1930 until its defeat in 1945, the most important economic and population centers of China had been occupied. Under the Chiang Kai Shek regime, warlordism prevailed.

From the years of the Long March, the base in Inner Mongolia and the armed struggle against the Japanese an outstanding group of leaders emerged at the head of the Chinese Communist Party—Liu Shaoqi who became president but Mao put him under house arrest for years; Deng Xiaoping, the party general secretary who was arrested by Mao but became the leader who broke with Maoism; Zhou Enlai who served as prime minister; Zhu De, the great military leader and others.

Unfortunately, Mao Zedong emerged by the late 1950s as the unchallengeable leader who pursued extreme policies and theories. China was going to skip the socialist stage and go straight to communism. Huge communes were formed and the economic laws of socialism abandoned for those of the communist stage. To catch up with the world capitalist level of production, steel was to be made in everyone's back yard. During the cultural revolution large numbers of people were persecuted for alleged bourgeois behavior. Great damage was done to agricultural production, contributing to widespread famine.

Before Mao's experiments with skipping stages, China had followed the Soviet model of economic and political structures, as did all the socialist countries including Vietnam and Cuba. After Mao's death and the political defeat of his immediate followers, there was a return to the Soviet model. But then under Deng Xiaoping 's leadership, China returned to Lenin's experience with the NEP and set out to experiment with the market model of constructing socialism.

In 1960 Mao openly broke the alliance with the Soviet Union. Mao followed an adventurous and nationalist policy that eventually led Mao's China into quietly siding with the U.S. and world imperialist drive against the Soviet Union and the nonaligned countries which were then led by India, headed by Indira Gandhi; Cuba, led by Fidel Castro; and Yugoslavia under Tito's leadership. The Maoists proclaimed that the basic contradiction was between the developed world (including the Soviet Union) and the developing world—not between the working class (including that section of it in power) and world imperialism. The revolution would be won by the countryside surrounding the cities. Armed struggle was the sole path. Mao said China was not afraid of world nuclear war because if China lost 100 million people in such a war they would still have 900 million people. Worldwide the Maoists played a negative role of splitting communist parties and the alliance of the working class, the developing countries and the peace movement. But as the extreme Maoists were defeated in China, to be replaced by the well-reasoned approach of Deng, the Maoist movement gradually disappeared in the rest of the world.

In recent years the growth rate of the Chinese economy has been as high as ever achieved anywhere in the world. The Chinese leadership says they have a plan to raise 100 million people out of poverty (by UN standards) every 10 years. They have completed that goal in the first 10 years and are in the middle of the second 100 million. They say they will complete raising the 1.3 billion Chinese people out of poverty in a century. They also say it will take them that long to construct socialism. What they have already achieved in relation to bringing nearly 150 million people out of poverty so far is unmatched in world history, and especially considering they came from one of the poorest, most backward countries in the world. They are now about the third largest economy in absolute terms but remain poor by per capita standards.

How has this come about and at what cost? The Communist Party remains the leading party. Since 1949 there have been eight other parties. In the early years they played a bigger role as coalition partners in the revolutionary process, but they are no longer a major force. The party leadership has proclaimed its intent to gradually increase democratic participation by the masses of the people in the life of the country, still under the Communist Party's leadership. The media, both Communist Party and not, express a wide range of debate on how best to overcome problems and move the country forward.

Having experienced years when the country was torn apart by other countries and then by warlords linked to Chiang Kai Shek, the Chinese are very concerned about the need for national unity and security. They worry that China could be easily torn apart again in an anarchist way in the absence of such security. This would be a great tragedy not only for the Chinese people but for the people of the world.

While the key industries remain nationalized, most of the economy consists of joint enterprises of one kind or another—the state with Chinese or foreign capitalists or the capitalists alone. There is also a growing sector of foreign capitalist-owned enterprises. But all of this operates under broad central planning by the state and with many regulations and restrictions over what the capitalists can do. When capitalist activity gets out of hand, new regulations are introduced. At present new laws are being put into effect strengthening the role of trade unions in protecting the interests of workers. The state, led by the Communist Party, continues to have the power to enact new laws that can completely dispossess capitalists who act in an extreme anti-social way.

Many criticisms have been made of specific policies and developments in China. In such a big country with such an immense population and complicated history, there are bound to be just criticisms from within the country and from outside observers. Many false criticisms have also been made by inveterate opponents of anything related to socialism. Sometimes friends of China make unfounded criticisms as a result of lack of knowledge of the totally different history and conditions. But a great social experiment, unprecedented in history, is bound to make important mistakes in the process.

China is now leading the way with a new path to socialism using a maximum of instruments from capitalism to increase production as fast as possible, in order to be able to raise living standards more rapidly and provide more social services completely free. So far they are showing that whenever a big social problem arises, the leadership takes it seriously and tries to do something about it. This is the case with the large migration from the countryside to the cities. Good standard apartment houses are being built on the outskirts of the cities to provide housing. Rural education and health services are being significantly upgraded. In order to overcome the lagging of the agricultural sector by giving peasants more incentive, new rights of transfer of land are being provided peasants, while residual ownership remains with the state. Since long before the revolution, China has had a huge environmental problem. The leadership singled this and poverty out as the two biggest tasks at the 2007 People's Congress. To give one example, the west has been surprised by the measures taken in relation to auto exhaust standards, which are superior to those of the capitalist powers.

The party takes a very serious attitude toward corruption, because it believes that corruption is the main factor that can undermine its leadership, and that the existence of a very large state capitalist sector greatly increases the risk of corruption. China has executed a number of officials for corruption. Many communist parties, including the CPUSA, oppose capital punishment for any purpose.

The Chinese leadership is also taking strong measures to improve quality and safety of products for both the internal and external markets.

China's exports have been diminished and its rate of growth has slowed under the impact of the world capitalist financial and economic crisis. China, however, is in a better position to cushion the impact through its planning and the level of government involvement in the functioning of the economy. It has already injected $600 billion into the economy to replace export demand with growth of the internal market and demand.

What China is trying to do is of great significance for all of progressive humanity. The issue is whether it can pursue this path without the internal and external forces of capitalism derailing the effort.

The Vietnamese revolution

Ho Chi Minh, Le Duan, Le Duc Tho, General Vo Nguyen Giap and the other Vietnamese Communists fought French, Japanese and U.S. imperialism from their party's founding in 1920 in Paris as part of the French Communist Party until they defeated the U.S. armed forces. Before defeating the U.S. they had surrounded and forced the surrender of the French at Dien Bien Phu. The relationship between the Vietnamese Communists, their allied political parties and the masses of people was remarkable. The exemplary role of "Uncle Ho" demonstrates that communism is not synonymous with the repressions and outlandish one-man decisions of Stalin and Mao.

The liberation war against the U.S. alone cost the lives of 3 million Vietnamese and 59,000 U.S. military. The chemical Agent Orange, tested by the U.S. on the Vietnamese, continues to take lives in both countries. The country has been successfully rebuilt and the economy is growing rapidly. The Vietnamese are using many of the same methods as the Chinese, although not making as extreme a use of capitalist investment. The popularity of the Communist Party, of socialism and Marxism remains high. The Vietnamese leaders also believe it will take some time to construct a socialist society.

The Cuban revolution

In 1959, the Batista semi-colonial regime was overthrown by the guerrilla army led by the July 26 Movement headed by Fidel Castro, Che Guevara, Raul Castro and others, and based in the Sierra Maestra Mountains. In the main cities, the Popular Socialist Party (Cuba's first communist party) had considerable strength among the workers and supported the Castro-led effort to overthrow Batista. The PSP was led by Blas Roca, Juan Marinella, Carlos Rafael Rodriguez and others, all of whom shared leadership in the second Communist Party created over the next few years out of the 26th of July Movement (which had a substantial Marxist current within it) and the PSP.

Cuba faced then and still faces the U.S. economic blockade. It was also a country without significant natural resources, and with a low level of industry. The economy was largely dependent on sugar and tobacco crops. Because of world economic developments, Cuba lost its ability to sell a big sugar crop abroad. The U.S. constantly threatened invasion. It tried to destabilize the country with the Bay of Pigs invasion. The Soviet effort to help Cuba defend itself against U.S. threats met a Kennedy administration that nearly set off a world nuclear war before calmer heads prevailed. The U.S. used internal sabotage, dissenters who stimulated periodic sizable boat exits to the U.S., attempts to assassinate Fidel Castro and other provocations.

Cuba has excelled in education and health care and in helping other countries with health care and the training of medical personnel. The collapse of the Soviet Union especially damaged the Cuban economy and social conditions. Every day two oil tankers had arrived from the Soviet Union to meet Cuba's needs. Now Cuba has found oil offshore and with the help of Venezuela and China is solving its energy crisis. Tourism has again become a major industry. Cuba is experimenting with some steps in the Chinese direction but it has not yet found a solution to build its economy rapidly and lift its standard of living.

While Cuba's democratic forms are not traditional and the Committees for the Defense of the Revolution have declined, there is no doubt the Communist Party and Fidel Castro and Raul Castro have maintained their popularity and Cuba, like Vietnam, has not suffered a crisis of democracy and leadership as did the USSR and some other countries of socialist orientation. Cuba, a small country of 11 million people, has played a big role in international affairs, as one of the founders of the Non-Aligned Movement, with its armed assistance to Angola, Namibia and South Africa in their liberation struggles, in its health care work, and in its influence on the development of other revolutionary movements in Latin America. Currently, a countrywide discussion is taking place as to what needs to be changed in the economy and political system to move forward faster.

Venezuela and the Latin American wave to the left

In recent years Venezuela, Bolivia, Nicaragua, Ecuador, Uruguay, Brazil, Argentina, Chile and Paraguay have seen various types and degrees of movement to the left. What they have in common is a rebellion against neo-liberalism, which destroyed government actions to benefit the masses and replaced them with austerity programs imposed by the International Monetary Fund (IMF) and transnational banks. These programs seriously hurt the living standards of the mass of people working on the land and the developing working class. In some countries the program offered as an alternative had populist and social democratic elements and liberal capitalist ideology. In others, there was a more radical, socialist and Marxist orientation often mixed with the rebellion of the indigenous majority against the more well to-do aristocracy and big landowning interests, as in Bolivia. There was also a demand to end foreign ownership and domination of the natural riches of countries like Venezuela and Bolivia.

The result has been various forms of political and economic cooperation. Venezuela, Bolivia, Nicaragua, Ecuador, and Cuba are working together both economically and politically and to defend their common interests against the efforts of the U.S. ultra-right government and other imperialist forces to disrupt and overthrow their governments. They have initiated cooperative arrangements such as oil for health care. A development fund has been formed as an alternative to the IMF and the World Bank including Brazil, Argentina, Uruguay, Paraguay, Bolivia, Ecuador, Venezuela and others.

Venezuela and Bolivia have declared that their objective is to construct socialism. Marxism is being studied in Venezuela's armed forces and a socialist party is being built there. It is not yet clear whether Marxism will become the dominant current in it, and the Communist Party of Venezuela is maintaining its separate identity while cooperating with the president and the new socialist party. In the recent state elections, the Communist Party supported the socialist party candidates in most states but ran its own candidates in two states, which led to a public rebuke by President Chavez.

Different mass community popular organizations of workers and others are being built. Venezuela defeated a U.S.-backed armed coup that aimed to keep oil out of the hands of the government and the people. The attempts of the industrial capitalist and agricultural oligarchy to overthrow the elected government of Hugo Chavez, to defeat it in elections and to preserve a monopoly of the mass media, all failed. The government is using its oil wealth to improve the living conditions of the poor majority, and to help other countries moving in the same direction. Venezuela is also providing heating oil to 50,000 poor families in the U.S. at reduced prices.

Each new experience with movement leftward toward socialism gives birth to radically different experiences, political movements, economic and social policies of development, combinations of class and social forces, and directions toward socialism and forms of its construction. Given the strength of U.S. resistance and that of other imperialist forces, the IMF and the transnational companies, some of these developments may be politically derailed or overthrown. This is also because the initial strength of Marxists and Marxist parties within the movements is relatively weak. But it can be expected that the variety of political and economic forms that move in this direction will grow with time, not only in Latin America but elsewhere in the world.

The variety will be ever greater and go well beyond the possibilities the great founders of Marxism considered and outlined. In Venezuela, the patriotic section of the military has played an important role. So has the personal relationship between Hugo Chavez and Fidel Castro. The necessary creation of a strong, mass, Marxist social-

ist party able to lead the working masses toward socialism in complicated, very difficult situations is again taking place in a unique, unex-
pected way as it did in Cuba. This will undoubtedly happen more and
more and the variations will be greater and greater and yet produce the
same law-governed result, the replacement of capitalism by socialism
with a Marxist, Communist Party playing the leading role, either
before or soon after the transfer of power, alone or for some time in
coordination with other left parties, and often alongside competing
parties opposed to socialism.

Lessons from building socialism under Stalin's leadership

What took place in the Soviet Union after Lenin? What lessons can
we learn from that experience?

At the 11th Congress of the Communist Party Lenin proposed
Stalin as the general secretary of the party. At the time of the 12th
Congress shortly before his death and when Lenin could not attend
the Congress, he addressed a letter to all the delegates proposing the
removal of Stalin because of the rude, intolerant way in which he
treated comrades. Lenin worried about this weakness in the person at
the top and what it would mean for Party unity. Stalin prevented the
letter from being delivered. At the Congress, Stalin claimed the man-
tle of being Lenin's successor, the person who would continue Lenin's
political and theoretical legacy.

First it should be noted that around Lenin were many Leninists, and
Leninism has well been characterized as the Marxism of the imperialist epoch. Leninism embraced an overall analysis and policy toward
imperialism and all major developments of the imperialist stage.
While others made practical and theoretical contributions, they could
only be considered Marxists by embracing and building on Leninism
as the continuation of Marxism in the new era.

The period under consideration ends with the collapse of the Soviet
state and socialism and a return to capitalism. It would be wrong to
conclude that because the first experience in the world with building
socialism made many mistakes, experienced some serious crimes, and
came to an end, it was a failure and accomplished nothing. The Soviet
experiment showed that:

• It was possible for the working class to take power and build a
socialist society. While this had been proven in theory, not until it
was accomplished in practice could the exploited and oppressed

masses of the world see that a better world was possible and they had the power to win it and build it.

• The Soviets set the pace that influenced all other countries in terms of social welfare programs for the masses of working people. These included free universal health care; free universal education through high school and free higher education for growing numbers; free day care for growing numbers of preschool children; government-financed pensions for the retirees in growing amount; growing networks of reduced-cost facilities for worker vacations and for retirees; provision of public housing at minimal rents; a substantial and rapid improvement in mass living standards and elimination of poverty and famine.

• Rapid development of the economy through industrialization, rapid scientific and technological development, great construction projects and rapid growth of labor productivity. These achievements were seldom matched elsewhere and showed the value of social ownership and economic planning. They made the USSR militarily competitive with Nazi Germany and proved highly beneficial to rapid reconstruction of the country and its economy in the aftermath of World War II.

• Most of the 100 formerly oppressed nationalities made rapid progress in catching up in living standards, culture, democratic rights and equality.

• The Soviets played the decisive role in saving humanity from fascism.

• The USSR played a crucial role in the defeat of colonialism and in helping the developing countries advance.

• It played a crucial role in the fight for peace and to prevent nuclear war.

• It played a very important role in the emergence of other socialist countries, some of which continue to the present time.

• It gave us rich experience of positive lessons on which to build, and what to learn about in order to avoid repetition of the negative.

Some of these successes in internal development began to slip backward after the early 1960s and especially after 1980. Agricultural production was never solved either in quantity, variety or cost of production. In industry, introduction of new technology and materials lagged, and costs of production failed to go down as expected. With respect to consumer goods, there were growing problems with variety and quality, and the costs of production failed to decline. As a result, in later years instead of the free services expanding in scope, coverage and quality, they tended to diminish or stagnate and it was never possible to provide substantial pensions for retirees. The housing stock deteriorated and diminished in relation to population size. Community property grew unattended. We shall discuss these issues further.

While many good things continued to happen in the development of national equality during Stalin's leadership, there were also crass violations of the lead Lenin had given on this question. Lenin had said the Jewish people had been the most oppressed under czarist Russia. Much progress had been made. And when the Nazis invaded Lithuania and Russia and effectively surrounded Leningrad and hundreds of thousands were starving to death, Jews were given first preference to be taken to the rear to avoid the Nazi exterminations. But then there were the arrests and executions of Jewish cultural figures and of the Jewish doctors in conjunction with the final illness of Stalin. And as the Nazis advanced, some peoples living in the Caucasus were moved to Central Asia on grounds their loyalty could not be depended upon.

Leninist principles on the national question were also violated in connection with the German-Soviet Non-Aggression Pact of 1938. It is understandable that the Soviet Union would make a non-aggression pact to gain time to prepare defenses against the expected attack by Germany. The Soviets had done everything they could to persuade Britain and France to join them in guaranteeing Poland and Czechoslovakia against attack by the Nazis, but without success. The Communist Party USA endorsed the Non-Aggression Pact but instead of continuing to predict Nazi aggression and recognizing its only purpose was to gain time for military preparations, the Pact was treated at face value. It turned out that the rumors of secret provisions were true. Germany and the USSR agreed on dividing Poland, the Baltic region and other neighboring territories, which violated principles of national relations. There is evidence Stalin began to have illusions in the trustworthiness of Hitler, despite Hitler's having placed the "Bolsheviks" as the main enemy in the world ever since "Mein

Kampf." The time gained by the Pact before the Nazis attacked was not used to make major military preparations and the Soviet Union was caught still unprepared when it was attacked.

Were the Stalin group's violations of Soviet legality and Leninist principles inherent in socialism as its opponents claim, or an anomaly of history? There are those who argue that given the developments in Russia—the repressive regime of the czars, the absolutist control by the czarist autocracy and the Russian Orthodox Church of the times, the lack of experience with liberal bourgeois democracy, the poverty and cultural backwardness, the surrounding of revolutionary Russia by hostile, interventionist powers, the threat of German fascism—the path followed was highly likely. But the path Stalin followed represented one trend among the Russian revolutionaries. Stalin was trained as a seminarian. Stalin developed a doctrine and practice that on many points departed from Leninism. His policies included successes, mistakes and crimes. Stalin was joined in this trend by Molotov, Kaganovich, Beria, Zhdanov, Vyshinsky and others.

That there would be such a political trend, given the background cited, is not surprising. That its adherents would succeed to the leadership following Lenin and his close associates was not at all inevitable or even likely. Lenin died relatively young because of the wounds from the would-be assassin some years before. Otherwise he might have lived longer and implanted a political system and culture befitting socialism. Lenin might have succeeded in his effort to remove Stalin from leadership at the 12th Congress. If the Congress had received Lenin's letter it is likely Stalin would have been replaced. There was a substantial opposition to Stalin in the party's leadership, in its Political Bureau, Central Committee and Congresses following Lenin's death. The opposition might have won out and replaced Stalin with something closer to Lenin's example. It took five years until 1929 for Stalin to remove all opposition from the Political Bureau. And Stalin still lost out on some issues at the 15th Congress in 1930.

It was not until 1934 at the 17th Congress, and finally at the 18th Congress in 1938 that Stalin was able to remove and imprison or execute half of the Central Committee and half of the General Staff, including the Chief of the General Staff, Marshal Tukhachevsky, as agents of German fascism or of other imperialist powers. Through the years the Stalin group grew from a political trend in the party making many errors of theory and practical policy into a fanatical clique. This group imprisoned or executed over 700,000 people (according to government and party reports in 1956 and 1988), most of whom they knew to be innocent, in order to produce what they considered a necessary atmosphere of vigilance against Nazi agents and to prepare to resist a German invasion and "save Russia and the revolution." Among the mass of people a cult of "the infallibility of Stalin" had been built up.

Some have explained what was done on the basis that Stalin was a paranoid personality and Beria, the person in charge of internal security, was a Western intelligence agent who played on the paranoia. Whether or not these assertions are true, it is clear from Molotov's memoirs and other evidence there was a group in the leadership that knew what they were doing but had become so fanatical in their politics that they considered their actions "necessary to save the revolution." Some acknowledge the crimes of Stalin but also attribute to him the successes in economic development and social conditions, and the defeat of fascism. There is more evidence to conclude these successes were achieved by the multi-million member Soviet Communist Party, the Soviet people and armed forces despite the Stalin group, rather than because of it.

After all, we know Stalin forced collectivization not only on the kulaks (rich farmers) but on the middle and poor peasants despite Lenin's prescription that these peasants be offered "bonuses" to join cooperatives. This proved a serious mistake for Soviet agriculture. Stalin denied the law of value in the socialist economy (see "Economic Problems of Socialism") leading to widespread violation of Marx's concept for the socialist stage of payment "according to work." This created work disincentives and commodity prices that often led to shortages and long lines. Stalin insisted on intervening in field after field in which he had no knowledge, resulting in great harm. Among these were biology where he supported Lysenko's theories over those of Michurin; physics where he declared the invalidity of quantum mechanics that proved necessary for cybernetics and computers; linguistics, which he assigned totally to the superstructure of class-divided society; music with his repeated criticisms of Prokofiev, Shostakovich and others; poetry where he criticized Mayakovsky repeatedly. Stalin's last speech to a Party Congress, the 19th in 1951, put forward as a universal law of development that once there is a socialist revolution the class struggle sharpens. This was a theory that provided a cover for his own actions and Stalin-inspired repression in other socialist countries.

The role of the Soviet Union in World War II was decisive. It was the main force to defeat Hitler fascism and the Axis powers at the terrible cost of 26 million dead and a ravaged country. Stalin was pictured as a military genius who saved the Soviet Union from fascism. But after he passed from the scene, the military leaders of the Soviet Union, Marshals Zhukov, Konev and Rokossovsky, all said in their memoirs that Stalin knew nothing of modern warfare and his interference nearly caused big catastrophies during the war.

Thus we conclude while the Stalin grouping was a product of specific, highly unusual conditions, it was not foreordained that it would become the leadership in Soviet Russia after Lenin. It was an anomaly of history that was in contradiction to the basic character of the socialist system. Communists who followed in the Soviet Union and other countries had and still have the task of providing greater guarantees that no such group can again garner such absolute power to violate the norms of socialist and communist party democracy. That is an ongoing task that has achieved results in the socialist countries and can be expected to achieve even greater results with more time and experience. In our country, our history and culture and level of development upon undertaking to construct socialism, and freedom from outside intervention, all give promise of avoiding what happened in the Soviet Union.

Lessons from the Soviet experience: 1953 until its demise

Stalin's death was followed by a difficult succession that finally came to Nikita Khrushchev in 1955. That led to the revelations in 1956 about how Stalin had led, which shocked nearly everyone in the world, including the Communist movement. This period was marked by more international peace initiatives by the USSR and a certain détente. The internal situation in the USSR seemed to open up wider expressions of opinion.

In 1962 Khrushchev proclaimed that the Soviet Union had reached the level of one-third the economy of the U.S. and that the socialist countries together had reached the level of two-thirds of world capitalism. He predicted that within 20 years, the USSR would surpass the

USA in per capita production. The Soviets also proclaimed that the Soviet Union would go over gradually from socialism to the communist phase in one area after another. Within the next few years Soviet theoreticians and political leaders found that the dictatorship of the proletariat was changing into the state of the whole people as there were no longer classes with contradictory interests but only cooperative classes that were beginning to merge into a classless society of the whole people.

Alongside the various nationalities of the Soviet Union a new formation of human community was coming into being, a single entity, the Soviet people. But there were evident difficulties not only in the Soviet economy but in that of other countries, including the most advanced like the German Democratic Republic and Czechoslovakia. Agriculture and consumer goods lagged badly and the growth rate of the economy as a whole had slowed. Agricultural experiments were tried in Central Asia, as was general decentralization of the economy, but they proved unsuccessful and were not fully implemented.

Brezhnev replaced Khrushchev in 1964. The criticism was made privately that Khrushchev was erratic and had not solved the economic problems. A broader economic reform of decentralization was agreed to in 1965 but never implemented.

The economic problems of the socialist countries were growing, and solutions had not been found. A reform trend emerged in Hungary associated with Hungarian party leader Janos Kadar and Soviet ambassador (later Soviet leader) Yuri Andropov. This trend experimented with decentralization and limited use of market forces in consumer goods. The reform movement existed in the Soviet Union, and in Czechoslovakia it was associated with party leader Alexander Dubcek. There it led to a crisis followed by the entry of Soviet military forces in 1968 to "save socialism." It is still unsettled whether Dubcek represented a search for legitimate reform or—like more extreme figures such as economic planning minister Otto Sik— sought restoration of capitalism. But in any case this was a setback for world socialism.

During the balance of Brezhnev's leadership and then Chernenko's brief term, there were no major developments, changes or solutions. When Andropov came in, the reformers, knowing his history in Hungary, hoped for some big changes. Those who opposed such change and felt the solution was more discipline and less corruption, knew his reputation as head of the KGB and expected the opposite direction. Andropov was also known as a theoretician and ideologist. His first moves were against drunkenness and for greater labor discipline. He had brought a reformer, Mikhail Gorbachev, to Moscow from the northern Caucasus to be responsible for agriculture, and the reformers expected Gorbachev to succeed Andropov.

After 18 months in office Andropov died and Gorbachev became the party and state leader in 1985. Who was responsible for what from this point on until the demise of the USSR and socialism remains unclear. There is no consensus in the world Communist movement and there may never be. Some extreme views should be rejected out of hand. The Soviet Union did not collapse because of the efforts of U.S. imperialism, even though U.S. imperialism was certainly at work at all times. It did not collapse because Gorbachev was an agent of U.S. imperialism. It is possible to judge all the initiatives he and the group around him took in different ways and find some of them useful to give socialism new life and some of them harmful. In 1984 the figures made available by the Soviet Government and party to the world movement showed an economy that had slowed in its growth rate but was not in serious trouble. When Gorbachev gave his first report to the Politburo in April 1985 he revealed those figures had been consciously falsified and that the situation was so bad that the economy was about to turn downward in absolute terms.

Our purpose here is not to assess Gorbachev and the other leading figures and trends of the time. It is enough to note that at first some relatively small economic reforms helped the economy and gained popular support. The aim was to follow that with an overall plan of economic reform. Several plans were brought in but due to infighting in the party leadership, all were rejected. At the same time, the economy declined, consumers were considerably worse off and public support dwindled both for the reformers and the party as a whole. The attempted coup of the old guard against Gorbachev and the reformers opened things up for a coup by Boris Yeltsin, then the leader of the Russian Republic, and by his associates who were out to restore capitalism and succeeded in doing so without any substantial public opposition.

What were some of the errors of theory and practice in the economy in the USSR and other European socialist countries that led them all to face an absolute decline in production and a loss of popular support? Why instead of catching up to the U.S. and the West in 20 years as Khrushchev predicted, did the USSR and the other countries fall further behind? What lessons do the socialist countries have to examine to avoid similar problems? Among them:

• The aim came to be to try and nationalize everything as fast as possible, viewing this particular form of social ownership of the means of production as the universal goal. This violated the concepts of Marx, Engels and Lenin. Collective farms were made virtually identical with state farms, ending material incentives from elements of market relations. This is one of several areas in which the estimate that the Soviet Union was ahead of where it actually was in terms of going over from socialism to communism hurt the economy. About 1950, all small businesses, repair services and small retail markets were nationalized. Since the economy was not prepared for that, the result was a collapse and closing of what had become state property overnight. Thus until its last days the Soviet Union was well known for its lack of repair facilities and consumer goods of quality or desirable style, while millions of shoes went unsold as undesirable.

• The Soviet Union became known for the poor quality of consumer goods and for poor quality and inefficiency of labor. This seems to have resulted from the tendency to level wages on the theory that the socialist motto of "from each according to his ability, to each according to his work" could be replaced by the communist motto "to each according to his need." In any case raises in pay, and pay according to performance, no longer had much impact as workers already had enough money to buy the little that was available to consumers and many consumer items, especially food, were already so low in price that the only result was longer lines.

• This raises the theoretical and practical question of the law of value under socialism. In Stalin's last work, "Economic Problems of Socialism," he claimed the law of value had very little role under socialism. This meant one could set prices arbitrarily to meet some desirable political goal without it causing any trouble. But when many consumer items were greatly undervalued, demand shot up and long lines resulted. Again the Kuusinen text theoretically rejected the concept that the law of value played little role under socialism as a form of "voluntarism"—ignoring objective reality because it does not conform to our wishes.

• The use of the market to stimulate production in quantity, quality and greater efficiency of production had long been rejected on theoretical grounds by the Soviet leadership and in much of the world Communist movement, as necessarily meaning a return to capitalism. While the logic of a completely uncontrolled market at all levels does go in the direction of capitalism, the experience and arguments of Lenin during the NEP were overlooked. With state power and the leadership of the government it was possible to set controls of the market so there might be competition in price, quality of production and costs of production at the levels desired and regulations could be changed when necessary. Experiments with the market in Hungary and elsewhere were looked at askance.

• A highly centralized system in which national administrative bodies decided everything by plan fed unwillingness to use the market at all and the absence of the market fed continued over-centralization. If individual plants were allowed to determine which commodities to produce and what prices at which to sell them, some local market competition might well result. When neither competition nor performance standards were required to secure necessary supplies from higher levels, and supplies were allotted simply by administrative directives, a premium was placed on the relationship between the factory manager and the administrator at the higher level. Relations of friendship, then of gifts and finally of corruption came to determine who got the most and best supplies first. Relations of administration and command took the place of economic relations, fostering widespread corruption. Over-centralization produced a whole bureaucracy at the ministry and trust level, at the all-Soviet level and then the republic level, before one got to the factory manager. This bureaucracy of close to 20 million people became a large political force resisting attempts at decentralization that would eliminate their jobs.

• Quotas set at the enterprise level for departments and work teams often did not have the intended effect. The object became to go just barely over the goal. If you did a good deal more, then you

could expect a major increase in your goal for the following year
without any commensurate reward (not to mention there was little
one could do with such a reward). So there was no reason to come
up with anything really big and new to greatly surpass the goal for
quantity of production or for saving input factors.

• The over-centralization fed a separation of production from
research and development. The Soviets were famous for their theoretical science and for discovering very useful processes that they
then had great difficulty in introducing into production. As a result
they tailed many others in production though they made the particular scientific discovery involved. These include cybernetics and in
steel, continuous casting. At the end, the USSR was way behind in
computers.

• There was the theory that the USSR could keep up with world
science and production even if it was cut off from the non-socialist
world economy. It was considered that full connection to that world
economy would lead to pressures to return to capitalism and to dan-
gers of espionage. Even efforts to end the isolation were often half-
hearted. While there were some risks, there was a gross underestimation of what was to be gained by strongly seeking participation.

• A full-blooded democratic political system and a socialist
economy are each necessary for the other. What we mean by a full-
blooded democratic political system was discussed under U.S.
socialism.

How could such mistakes have been made in the realm of the economy, democracy and the political system, and national relations?

After all, there were millions of people and their leaders who set
out to build something new in human history, a qualitatively better
society, a socialist society. They were armed with the Marxist ideology of the working class. But it was uncharted territory, an historical
experiment. And as we discussed, it was undertaken in one of the most
backward of the great powers. Russia's economy was very backward
and its cultural level was backward in terms of education, as well as
the repressive experience of the czarist regime and the Russian
Orthodox Church of that time. The Soviet Union existed under
extremely difficult conditions, alone and surrounded by the capitalist

powers that wanted to kill it militarily or strangle it economically, or annihilate it by fascist military means and then with atomic bombs.

The Soviet Union lost its great leader, Lenin, when he and the great experiment were relatively young. Lenin did not succeed in assuring his succession by someone in the same mold and with the same political policy. That Lenin did not live another 20 years and did not succeed in removing Stalin from leadership before he died are accidents of history. There could well have been a different course of development. Stalin turned out to be an abomination for the Soviet Union and the world communist movement.

A pattern was set in theory and policy that though greatly ameliorated under those who followed Stalin, still affected the economic and political structure and culture to a considerable degree and prepared the downfall and the end of Soviet socialism in that period. But as we have seen, the socialism that so far has followed, has learned lessons both from the Soviets' successes and their failures.

What lessons can be drawn from the experiences in winning and constructing socialism so far in world history? Capitalism can be replaced and be followed by nothing other than the construction of socialism. The winning of power is very complicated and difficult. The effort requires and is capable of winning support of the widest combination of popular forces. Both before and after the change in political power, an active majority supporting the change is decisive. This majority must be activated and drawn into making and carrying out all the major decisions of the new power. This democratic process may well involve more than one party of socialism and parties not yet won to socialism or even opposed to it.

Winning and sustaining power requires a Marxist party with great mass influence to shape the proper strategy and tactics, the proper social measures and the proper first steps in the economy. It requires the leadership of the working class or its active support to win the change of power and then its leading role to uphold it. All these things can take place in a great variety of forms. Very strong resistance can be expected from the national and world ruling class forces. The construction of an actual socialist society takes a lengthy period of time, even when socialism can be and is declared immediately to be the goal. It takes time to win wavering sections and to reach the stage of development of the forces of production that they will support predominant socialist class relations. The political and economic forms to accomplish that are endless in possible variety and combination. And time will constantly produce an even greater variety of the expression of these basic necessities for progress and socialism. In the great variety of paths to socialism, and the uniqueness of each model, what then is common to every socialist society that justifies calling each "socialist" is some form or forms of social ownership and working people's power led by the working class.

Whatever difficulties are experienced in building socialism, they can and must be overcome for the forward march of humanity to continue and triumph.

5 Getting There from Here: The Theory of Socialist Revolution

The theory of strategy

Once the study of the political economy of capitalism and historical materialism has shown that the great ills of our time stem from the destructive nature of capitalism, what comes after capitalism? Is there a way out and forward for humankind? We have answered that socialism comes next and it is decidedly a way forward for humankind. Then the issue is how to go from where we are to working-class-led power to build a socialist society in the U.S. How to go from where we are, all the way to socialism, Lenin termed the "theory of socialist revolution." In turn it consists of two major aspects, the theory of strategy and tactics, and the theory of the party of the new type. Still another aspect deals with the need for other types of organizations, the trade unions and the Young Communist League.

From "The Communist Manifesto" on, in every work dealing with class, democratic and social struggles, Marx and Engels dealt with strategy and tactics but never by such labels, nor much in terms of a

117

theory of strategy and tactics. Rather it was a matter of what strategy
and tactics were called for in different situations, without using those
terms. As early as 1897 Lenin began discussing the need for a democratic stage of the Russian Revolution before the proletarian, socialist
stage. In his great work, "Two Tactics of Social Democracy in the
Democratic Revolution" (1905), Lenin discussed two stages necessary in the Russian Revolution but called them "tactics" rather than
the later language of "strategy." In 1920 Lenin produced another great
work, "'Left-Wing' Communism, An Infantile Disorder: A Popular
Essay in Marxian Strategy and Tactics." But nowhere in the text are
the words "strategy and tactics" defined and they are mentioned but
once. In 1935, at the 7th Congress of the Communist International,
General Secretary Georgi Dimitrov delivered his famous report calling for the building of a united front of the working class and a people's front of the working class and other class and social strata to
defeat world fascism. These objectives were termed a new tactic,
though today we would call them the new strategy of that period.

So what is strategy and tactics? It is a guide to action how to move
closer and closer to winning power and building socialism. It is based
on science, but tactics especially is primarily "art." By art we mean
being able to combine experience in struggle with an ability to pick
the most useful forms of struggle and forms of organization; select the
key issues of struggle and formulate well the appropriate demands.
All these involve skills and experience as well as a grasp of principles
of tactics—a subject we shall discuss. Strategy rests on a knowledge
of the laws of social development and political economy.

What is the stage of social development that a given country has
reached? Are there any stages of social development a given country
must still pass through before the issue becomes direct transition to
socialism? Are there remainders of prior social systems in the given
country which must be taken into account in determining the strategic
policy? Once the strategic goal is determined that will shift the balance of forces, it is necessary to determine accurately, by science, the
objective interests of different class and social forces in relation to that
strategic goal. Which class and social forces can be won to fight for
that strategic goal and what will need to be their relationship to each
other, which one will be the leading force for progress? Who will be
the main opponent and who are that opponent's possible allies? On

such issues, you are either right or wrong, sound or unsound from a scientific analysis of the situation, though it is possible that practice may prove you have inaccurately assessed the objective situation and drawn wrong strategic conclusions, which must then be corrected.

In 1924 Stalin wrote an essay on strategy and tactics that became a chapter in the longer work, "Foundations of Leninism," which for many years was used to discuss the theory of strategy and tactics in the U.S. and world Communist movement. In it Stalin characterized both Marxist strategy and tactics as matters of science. He also defined Marxism as a whole as science. But since the Soviet textbook "Fundamentals of Marxism-Leninism" (1960), to which we referred earlier, Stalin's concepts have been considered unsound and harmful. Tactics often require trial and error to see what works best in bringing to life the strategic policy of the Communist movement. Tactics can be unsuccessful as well as successful. They might need changing. By including all of Marxism as science, including all of the tactics used in every struggle, tactics were made unassailable as *always* correct, and to oppose them when they were put forward by a Stalin was to depart from Marxist science and the outlook and interests of the working class.

Strategy and tactics are now characterized as both science and art, and Marxism-Leninism is characterized as the "outlook" or "ideology" of the working class, rather than as containing nothing but scientifically true propositions. As Engels often said, Marxism is "a guide to action," not an infallible "scientific" dogma.

Strategy can deal with the overall socioeconomic stage of development in a country or a stage of struggle short of that, which when won, would change the relationship of forces in the country as a whole. Marx, Engels and Lenin all looked for something short of the socialist revolution, the winning of which would shift the balance of forces in a more favorable direction, making it easier to advance toward the proletarian revolution. For Marx and Engels in "The Manifesto," a stage of struggle in their native Germany that would open the path to larger qualitative change included alliance with the Democratic Party of Germany (a party of the rising capitalist class) in order to gain support to overthrow feudalism in Germany. But they sought such alliance with the small working class playing the leading role and then if successful, sought to avoid going through the full building of capitalism before they could go on to the struggle for a working-class-led revolution to construct socialism.

Lenin also looked for an objectively existing difference in interests, and a possible stage that would weaken the czarist autocracy; a stage that, having been won in a certain way, would open up the ability to move on to the further stage and strategic objective of a working class, socialist revolution. In 1897 and then in "Two Tactics" in 1905, Lenin proposed fighting for a democratic stage to defeat the autocracy, with the working class leading the way and including the peasants as a whole, while neutralizing the role of the rising capitalist class. If achieved, that would open the path to a second stage under the leadership of the working class, in alliance with the poor peasantry and against the capitalist class, to construct socialism. Such was Lenin's concept of strategy and strategic stages.

The theory of strategy and tactics can also be applied to a struggle in a city or state, dealing with the overall relationship of forces there, or with a single issue. It can also be applied nationally to a single issue of struggle. In working out strategy, the first question is: what is the strategic goal which, if won, will change the relationship of forces and open up the possibility of moving to a more advanced strategic goal? Once that strategic goal or objective is defined, then it is possible and necessary to determine the main opponent and possible allies of that opponent, based on an assessment of their objective interests. Then it is crucial to determine what forces have self-interest in fighting for that strategic goal, what can and should be the leading force in that struggle and what allies can be won. This is the strategic line or policy to win the strategic goal. It is sometimes called the "policy" or "line" of the Communist Party, to fight for the strategic goal against the strategic enemy on the basis of the determined strategic alliance, with the strategic leader (usually the working class).

When the strategic goal deals with a particular issue in a more limited area like a single city, the level of consciousness and activity of different class and social forces, movements, organizations and political tendencies plays a bigger role. This is in addition to the assessment of objective class and social group interests in determining who is the opponent and who can be won to fight for the strategic objective. In such situations both the objective and the subjective factors need to be taken into account because when the time span and other aspects are more limited, what already exists plays a bigger role compared to what is possible and likely in the longer run.

Winning the strategic goal or objective and changing the balance of forces are usually one and the same thing. In class-divided society, achieving any strategic goal involves qualitatively changing the alignment of forces that supports what exists. It usually takes a lot of time to build the needed strategic alliance in sufficient numbers to change the balance of forces and win a national strategic goal. Sizable forces, including many who are confused about their real interests, have been supporting the more backward, existing balance. It takes a long time to clarify and assemble sufficient forces to change the balance. It is important to make an accurate assessment of the existing balance of forces in order to avoid overestimating or underestimating the forces on either side.

What and who are the forces on the other side? Why are they on that side and how solidly? What and who is on your side to begin with why and how solidly? What additional forces are needed and how hard is it likely to be to win them? As we shall see, in the U.S., the forces for each change in a progressive direction include the working class in the lead, in close alliance with the nationally and racially oppressed, women and youth. Forces for progressive change also include other class and social forces, movements and political tendencies according to the strategic goal and the concrete change sought in the balance of forces. This is a matter of their objective self-interest and how the relation of forces has actually been developing.

When the objective is to change the balance of forces around a single issue nationally or at city or state level, the balance of forces may be less long-lasting and stable to begin with and easier to change. But care is still needed in estimating it. Again the subjective side of political understanding, consciousness and organization plays a bigger role and must enter into the estimate of the existing balance of forces and what it will take to win a qualitative change in the desired direction. But it can be safely said that in all situations winning the maximum of the working class, the racially and nationally oppressed, women and youth and their unity will determine the ability to change the balance of forces and win the strategic objective. This is at the heart of bringing into life the strategic alliance that is possible and necessary. In the U.S. the working class together with the racially and nationally oppressed, women and youth are considered the "core forces" for social change. That is because of the oppression they all experience, together with the exploitation their working-class sectors suffer. It is because of the size and potential power of these forces and that they are strongly intertwined. Thus by interests and power, together they constitute the core forces for progressive social change.

During our Civil War, Marx and Engels followed events closely. Marx wrote a number of articles on the subject. These were published by a Vienna newspaper and by the "New York Daily Tribune," the most widely-read newspaper of the times, read by Lincoln and the leading abolitionists, radicals and Marxists. Lincoln eventually pursued the strategy they urged to win the Civil War. For Marx and Engels, the strategic goal was a revolutionary one, to defeat the slavocracy and reunite the country with slavery gone. The strategic alliance they projected included the slaves and the freemen and women of the North, the rising industrial capitalists of the North, the newly developing working class, the abolitionists and radicals. They also believed it was necessary to gain the support of the militant working class of England and France to prevent the English and French industrial capitalist classes from bringing those countries into the war on the side of the Confederacy. Those capitalists had reason to support the Confederacy in order to guarantee their supply of slave-produced cotton for their manufacturing industries by ending the North's blockade.

Marx and Engels played a substantial role in helping win the English and French working classes to oppose slavery and side with the North, despite great hardship they suffered as a result of reduced production and closed factories. To achieve the strategy outlined, Marx and Engels opposed the entry of Missouri and Kansas into the Union as slave states. If that had occurred the slaveholders would have achieved control of the Senate. Joseph Weydemeyer, a co-worker of Marx, and other refugees from the defeated German Revolution of 1848, were numerous in Missouri and played a big role in preventing the slaveholders from winning there. Weydemeyer became a major in the Union Army.

Marx called for the immediate emancipation of the slaves and their enlistment in the Union Army. After these measures were adopted and this revolutionary strategy put into life, the Civil War was won.

Frederick Douglass and his associates and the Radical Republicans played the major role in pushing and supporting Lincoln to put this strategy into life.

Unfortunately, major aspects of the victory were betrayed with the Hayes-Tilden "Compromise" of 1876. Jim Crow was left in place until the Civil Rights revolution of the 1960s and not fully completed even then in the country as a whole.

Strategy is not self-implementing. It is like a plan on a piece of paper. It includes the strategic goal, the balance of forces to be changed, the strategic opponent(s), the alliance to be built for victory, including which class or social force is to lead in alliance with which other core forces and other potential allies. The strategy is either sound or unsound. If put into life, sound strategy is capable of winning. Only one strategy can be sound for the goal in the same political period. Whether the strategy is transformed from a theoretical plan on paper to something developing in life depends on its soundness and its tactical implementation in the most useful way.

Tactics

The strategic policy comes to life only through tactics. What issues need to be put forth to advance the strategy? What demands? What are the best forms of struggle, whether a mass demonstration in Washington, D.C., demonstrations in as many cities and towns as possible on a given date? Messages and visits to members of Congress, vigils, house meetings, sit-ins, civil disobedience, a mass petition, a general strike? What forms of organization are needed to encompass all the forms of struggle—a national membership organization, a coalition with many member groups, a coalition of coalitions of different constituencies and issues, informal consultations? And so on.

The test is what combinations of these will most successfully bring the strategic alliance into being with the leading forces in place on the widest basis for the strategic goal. The objective is to select the issues, demands, forms of struggle and forms of organization that will narrow down the opponent to the minimum and enlarge the strategic alliance sought, especially in terms of the maximum numbers of the core forces of labor and the working class, the nationally and racially oppressed, women and youth.

Generally tactics change relatively rapidly and strategy lasts until the strategic objective and change in the balance of forces is achieved.

Tactics are to be judged by effectiveness: do they succeed well in bringing into life the strategy sought? Experience in how given tactics succeed is key to their continuation, modification or complete abandonment. The strategic policy continues until the strategic goal and balance change is won.

Some people on the left confuse strategy and tactics. If something that is tactical is treated as if it were strategic, the result is rigidity, a failure to change tactics with circumstances or to learn from trial and error. A fetishism of forms of demands, forms of struggle and organization leads to tactical isolation and narrowing down and thereby loss of the ability to win the strategic goal. On the other hand, failure to have a strategy or treating what is strategic as if it were tactical results in loss of any real direction to the struggle. There is no quantitative development of the struggle leading to qualitative development, to more advanced stages. Instead, there is aimlessness, repetition of prior stages, and the development of pessimism, defeatism, and sometimes adventurism. In the case of tactics it is sometimes possible and desirable to pursue more than one tactical form, or combinations, at a time.

As distinguished from other approaches to strategy and tactics, the Marxist approach stresses the class and social forces, as well as political tendencies present, a careful estimate of these, and seeking qualitative shifts in the balance of forces, or turning points, to enable further advance. It stresses tactics that will move those class and social forces, especially the working class and nationally oppressed in their millions.

U.S. application of the theory of strategy

The Communist Party USA's application of the theory of strategy concludes that there are three possible stages to reach socialism. Each of these represents objectively existing changes that have taken place. None are simply convenient divisions into arbitrary slices. As discussed in Chapter 2, internationalization of economic life under capitalism led to changes in the relations of production within the framework of capitalism. Transnational corporations became the dominant form of capitalist ownership. That led to the emergence of an especially reactionary, ultra-right political trend based in a section of the transnationals. With the collapse of the Soviet Union and other European socialist countries, the U.S. had clear military dominance. These transnationals, particularly those based in armaments and energy but also among pharmaceuticals and sections of other industries such as banking, finance, high tech and even marketing (Wal-Mart) called for the U.S. to use military superiority to achieve its aggressive economic and political objectives in the world. They favored unilateralism in foreign policy. They launched the invasion of Iraq and have refused to end the war even when it was clear the U.S. could not win it.

The policy of this ultra-right grouping included severe limitations of democratic rights, big tax cuts for transnational monopoly capital and commensurate reductions in spending for social welfare measures. The policy of the ultra-right transnationals also includes a strong attack on affirmative action and attempts to divide the country using racism and anti-immigrant sentiment. The standard of living stagnated or declined for most working people. This sector of the transnationals gained dominance in the Republican Party and drew together a mass base of religious conservatives, nativists, social conservatives, libertarians, people in the exurbs of big cities, in small cities and towns particularly in the South and West, and even limited support in other areas of the country. They won the presidency in 1980, '84 and '88, and in 2000 and 2004. In 2000 they also controlled the Congress, the judiciary and many state governments, until the Congressional and state elections of 2006.

The other section of the transnationals was more willing to make concessions to working people. It dominated the Democratic Party. The bulk of the labor movement and working class, the African American, Latino, Asian and Jewish voters, women and youth have constituted the mass base of the Democratic Party. It was dominated nationally by centrist forces but by progressives in some areas. As a whole the Democratic Party consists of centrists, progressive and left forces as well as some rightists. Even the centrist representatives of the more moderate and realistic sector of the transnationals favored a less militarily aggressive, more collaborative foreign policy, and concessions to the various sections of its base on issues such as social welfare programs and racism.

Given these objective realities, the strategy for the initial stage has been to defeat the ultra-right, making the sharpest focus on the Bush administration and the Republican Party in power, and the related sector of the transnationals. To accomplish that has required an all-people's front led by labor and based on close alliance of the core social forces of the working class, the racially and nationally oppressed, women and youth. But the all-people's front also includes middle strata and even the section of the transnationals opposed to the ultra-right and operating through the Democratic Party. It includes the peace movement and other progressive social movements and the political tendencies of centrist, progressive and left forces, the great bulk of whom operate through the Democratic Party. Thus the strategy or strategic policy during the first strategic stage, a stage of struggle, is to defeat the ultra-right, to drive them from governmental power by building an all-people's front led by labor in close alliance with the other core forces. The all-people's front is not a unitary organizational form but is rather a very loose coalition of organizations and forms that operates more in parallel than by formal agreement.

The process of moving from the anti-ultra-right to the succeeding anti-monopoly stage of struggle can be accomplished in more than one way. There is no single, firm, precise, discreet line of separation between these two stages. The bigger the mass movement for ending the dominance of the ultra-right and for advanced democratic, antimonopoly demands expressing themselves in the electoral arena through advanced candidates and forms that can and do win out, the more complete will be the defeat of the ultra-right. Its control over all aspects of life can be swept away relatively quickly, leaving few vestiges with which an advanced majoritarian anti-monopoly movement will have to contend. The stronger such a movement, the more it will come into leading positions in government, able to implement not only measures to clear out the ultra-right but also to begin to curb the power of the transnational monopolies as a whole.

Defeating the ultra-right narrowly with a program, movement and candidate(s) relatively less advanced, would leave the ultra-right still influencing this or that, even if defeated overall. And it would mean only halting steps to take on monopoly as a whole.

The 2008 election

In the election of Barack Obama as president by a big margin with an increased Democratic margin in both Houses of Congress, and with victories in state elections, the anti-ultra-right strategy for the present stage has been realized. Of course, life never develops exactly like our strategic plan on paper. The ultra-right has lost control of the executive and legislative branches. This was accomplished by a very loose coalition of the core forces previously outlined and by many people from other sections of the population.

Labor voted for Obama by 69%. The African American vote was 96%, Latinos 68%, Asian Pacific Islanders 61%, Jews 78%, women 54%, youth 66%, and white people of all classes supported Obama by 44% to McCain's 54%. About 32 million white people voted for the first African American president. The moderate (centrist) and progressive political trends united in support of Obama.

The process of transformation from the anti-ultra-right stage to the anti-monopoly stage is underway. This involves completing the defeat of the ultra-right and restoring much that they had destroyed and steadily, in field after field, moving on to fighting for demands at the expense of monopoly as a whole, radically curbing its power. To accomplish this requires widening and deepening the unity of the core forces and adding ever-increasing sections of working people, while losing as few of the leading centrists who have close ties with monopoly, as possible. The vast movement in this direction is led by Barack Obama and thus those who have differences and/or seek to overcome past difficulties must keep in mind to do so in such a way that it does not play into the hands of reaction and others who want to split the unity now centered around President Obama.

The election of the first African American president strikes an important blow for equality and against racism. It creates a new plateau from which to continue this struggle which remains central to the whole struggle for democracy and progress. The African American people and all the specially oppressed peoples continue to live in greatly inferior conditions in every aspect of life. While the prospects for continually moving ahead and completing the transition to the anti-monopoly stage of struggle look promising, it cannot be predicted with complete certainty that there will be no temporary break. Any such break, however, would be temporary as this is a necessary development that objectively weakens capitalism as a whole and is part of the necessary path to socialism.

The anti-monopoly strategic stage

In his book "The Twilight of World Capitalism" (1949), William Z. Foster, then chairman of the Communist Party USA, introduced a new strategic concept to the CPUSA and the world Communist movement.

He argued that differentiation had developed among the capitalists. The monopoly capitalists had come to dominate the economic and political world of capitalism. This created the potential to win additional sectors of the population to ally with the working class for the purpose of severely weakening the harmful domination of the monopolies. A coalition could be built to radically curtail the economic, political and ideological power of the monopoly capitalists. Such a coalition would need to be led by the working class and have a close alliance with the nationally oppressed, at that time clearly the "Negro people" in the first place. The anti-monopoly coalition would include all the nationally oppressed, women, youth, the middle strata of self-employed, ("free") professionals, small business people and family farmers. The middle-sized capitalists could be neutralized so they would not side with the monopolies but they could not be counted on as allies against the monopolies.

This strategic concept became the position of the CPUSA and other parties in the developed capitalist world and was accepted by the whole world Communist movement. Some argued at the time, however, that the anti-monopoly stage was not a necessary stage of social development and only postponed moving on to the stage of the direct struggle for working-class power and building socialism. But the CPUSA concluded the fight for the anti-monopoly coalition, which included the fight to build a mass people's party led by the working class and not including any sector of monopoly, would open up the path to socialism. It would seriously weaken capitalism as a whole and it would open the possibility of a transition to socialism without civil war.

Since the development of transnational monopolies and the differentiation within the transnationals of an ultra-right section, defeating this section has become the immediate strategic objective, which then creates the possibility to build the coalition against the transnational monopolies as a whole the "anti-monopoly" stage of struggle. Such a coalition, with the strategic goal of radical democratic reforms at the expense of the transnational monopolies as a whole, would include the forces Foster outlined. The core allies of the working class would be the racially and nationally oppressed as a whole, women and youth and then all the other class and social forces he listed. In addition to the African American people the nationally oppressed include especially the Mexican American people and Latinos generally, Native American Indians, East and South Asians and Pacific Islanders, Arab and other Middle Eastern peoples. The coalition should seek to include the peace movement, and all the social issue movements and political tendencies including at least a section of centrists, as well as the progressives and the left. As argued, it can be even bigger and involve a wider array of forces as higher percentages of the working class, the nationally oppressed, the middle strata and others become convinced capitalism needs radical reform, and that the power of the transnational monopolies as a whole needs to be seriously curbed. As a people's anti-monopoly party is built, such a strategic objective becomes increasingly evident and possible.

As Foster argued, a successful anti-transnational monopoly coalition that does in fact radically curb its power will open the road to the next strategic goal, the direct struggle for working peoples' power under the leadership of the working class for the purpose of being able to construct a socialist society.

The socialist strategic stage and goal

The change from the first strategic stage, goal and policy to the second, anti-monopoly one will not be a perfectly clear crossing of a line; there will be some intertwining before the passage from one into the other is more or less complete. But in advancing from the antimonopoly stage to the socialist stage, there is a more or less consistent line to be crossed, a change in class power and the construction of a new socioeconomic formation. The strategic objective is working people's power, led by the working class, to construct socialism. The strategic allies to accomplish that and to share in power under work-ing-class leadership are all the working people, starting with the working class and the other core forces. Other working people include family and small farmers, self-employed, professionals, small business people in the cities and rural areas the entire middle strata. Again because of the continued experience with capitalism such that broader masses from all sectors of the population become more convinced that capitalism really does not offer them anything except great social problems, the majority for this coalition should be even larger, ready for a real, lasting solution to the great social ills. The coalition will need a large left, a large socialist component and a mass Communist Party with very wide influence. The latter requirement will be discussed in the chapter on the Communist Party. Why such a coalition growing out of the anti-monopoly stage will have the capacity to win state power without civil war and is quite likely to succeed in that effort, has been discussed in Chapter 3, **Historical Materialism**.

We have been discussing strategic stages to socialism. That is strategy. But it will not leave the realm of theory without being put into life through struggle and tactics such as issues, demands, forms of struggle and of organization. Marxism does not leave us empty-handed in deciding tactics. There are principles of tactics, developed out of the experience of past struggle, to help guide us.

Principles of tactics

Tactical principles help us choose the tactic or combination of tactics that are likely to be most successful in realizing the strategy sought. These principles are taken primarily from the writings of Lenin and from recent experience in using Marxist methodology.

- Lenin says for the millions to develop political consciousness it is necessary for them to have their own experience in social struggle for progress. To gain that experience, the main level of activity has to be the level on which masses are currently prepared to struggle, to act. That is the mass action or organization level—the level of issues and demands, of forms of struggle and organization that the broadest masses are currently ready to utilize. Lenin argues that propaganda and agitation are also necessary and helpful but by themselves will never bring about major change.

Propaganda for "socialism" for the full solution of the social problem that is being addressed, for the strategic goal to be won is necessary so that the number of people on the left who consider these solutions desirable and necessary, and the number joining the Communist Party and YCL, will grow. These forces will help move the millions who are on the action level. There also is a need for agitation which prepares the masses currently in motion to go on to the next stage of struggle. To engage primarily or exclusively in propaganda and agitation or to undertake actions or goals not tied in to the main issues, is a sectarian error that isolates from the masses and cannot long attract masses of people. Such an approach loses the confidence of the people and leads to questioning whether you are "for real" and what your real agenda is. People who approach everything very abstractly and intellectually often overemphasize propaganda and agitation. While treating the action level of masses as primary, a failure to engage in propaganda and agitation will lead to liquidating the most advanced forces including the Communist Party and to a loss of political course for the mass movement so that it is unable to develop from one point and stage to another.

- Another principle is to take into account whether the general period of mass activity is one of flow, or ebb. Issues, demands, forms of struggle and organization change in appropriateness and success according to that reality and our correct assessment of it. All movements in the country as a whole or on a particular issue like peace, or in a particular area of the country have periods of both ebb and flow. It is important to understand that both are inevitable and cannot be eliminated by the force of desire or effort. They become objective factors. They are expressions of the law of uneven development. There is not an even, constant forward march in the struggle for progress. The struggle is too complex for that and as Lenin points out, the level of social consciousness necessary to approach that will not be achieved until the stage of a communist society. Only then will the millions reach a level of social consciousness and of continuous participation in socially responsible activity that reduces the "ebbs" in forward movement.

In a period of ebb, tactics will consist more of teach-ins, town meetings and vigils rather than mass demonstrations. These are aimed at preparing the thinking of masses to go over to a period of flow. The ebb and flow concept emphasizes an important point about tactics. They have to be highly flexible.

- Knowing how to retreat is a necessary part of tactics. Retreat is closely related to ebb and flow, and to making a sober estimate of the actually existing relation of forces. Sometimes the existing relation of forces is highly unfavorable, and not because of the mistakes of the people's forces. The people's forces often do not control major circumstances and so are confronted with a choice of trying to advance when defeat is highly likely, or retreating. Then it is necessary to know how to retreat in good order, preserving the main democratic and progressive forces for the next period when advance becomes possible, in part because of the skill with which the retreat was handled.

Refusal to recognize the necessity to retreat and acting as if advance and a period of flow still exist can lead to bigger losses and dispersal of the democratic and progressive forces. Recognition of the necessity to retreat at times leads to conducting the struggle in terms of issues, demands, and forms of struggle and organization that prepare the forces for progress to be able to go over to advance when a new period of flow begins to emerge. Knowing when it is necessary to retreat and how to do it helps prevent demoralization, extreme discouragement, defeatism, paralysis, dispersal and adventurism. It helps prepare the way to a new period of advance when that becomes possible. At the national level, over a substantial period of time, there will be periods that require retreat alongside those that permit advance. Advancing or retreating is not a matter of mood or simply deciding on an attitude. It is a response to an objective estimate of the existing relationship of forces. One can retreat in response to such an unfavorable relationship of forces with a spirit that says, we'll be back, but the attitude of not being downcast does not change the objective fact of retreat.

• It is also a fact that there will be victories and periods of advance on the road to socialism. Any concept that sees only defeats of the working class and its allies is wrong and harmful. There are those on the left who fear victories and even deny their existence. They fear that victories produce illusions and acceptance of the existing situation and unwillingness to pursue more advanced goals. They fear it builds reliance on leading figures and their organizations who do not want to go further or are simply riding the tide for their own narrow, exploitative interests. But failure to recognize victories, even quite partial ones, is to deny that the working class and its allies have the ability to understand their own power when they are united and engage in mass struggle. Marx, Engels and Lenin discussed the necessity for the working class to become fully class conscious and understand its own potential and necessary role as the consistent leader in the struggle for progress and socialism. Recognizing real advances is also necessary to assess the existing relationship of forces and what can be done to advance the struggle still further. With a consistent working-class outlook it is still possible to over- or underestimate what has actually been won and what stage has been reached, but further developments will clarify the estimate. But having such a working class outlook anchors the judgment of where temporary allies are and what is their role in further developments in the stages of struggle leading to socialism. Fearing to recognize victories underestimates what is possible and slows down the forward movement of core forces on new terrain.

- Fetishism of tactics. A related concept is Marxism's opposition to fetishism of tactics. This approach treats tactics as though they were strategy, namely, as being sound without change over a long period of time. Making a matter of tactics into strategy has been tried many times over the years in many countries and caused much harm. In the U.S. the Industrial Workers of the World (IWW) called for "one big union" and for a general strike regardless of time, place and circumstance. Today there are leftist groups who always want to move from first actions to a nationwide general strike. There were the syndicalists and anarchists who wanted to put entities such as the utopian communities in the place of the state. Staughton Lynd and others once favored going from here to social revolution by establishing bases in the countryside in order to surround the cities, mechanically copying the forms of the Chinese Revolution.

Several ultra-left groups now make a fetish out of a particular form of struggle, such as armed struggle or non-conventional military struggle. In their view, anything less cannot achieve major social change anywhere in the world. They say that armed struggle is to be supported wherever it has some semblance of representing or involving the have-nots against imperialism or its servants.

Armed struggle is a form of struggle. It is tactical and must fit the needs of achieving the necessary strategic alignment of forces. But if it is treated as strategy, this means a loss of direction and an inability for it to serve the needed strategy. Using it as strategy prevents flexible changes of tactics based on whether in practice it helps achieve the alignment of forces required to gain the strategic objective. The issue of an oppressed people choosing these means to seek freedom, and the new issues of nuclear war and civilians as targets, are discussed in Chapter 3, **Historical Materialism.** The expression, "Anything but electoral forms of struggle" also treats tactical forms as though they are strategy, without flexibility. Some groups can be counted on to propose a big mass demonstration in Washington, D.C. in October of election years to prevent "illusions" about participating in "electoral politics." Others make a fetish of trashing a downtown area or particular buildings of state authority, hoping to interfere with the functioning of the state or the system to the point where "concessions will be forced." The fact that such tactics will be rejected by most working people and narrow the needed strategic alliance matters not to them. Some also insist that civil disobedience is the only moral and/or effective form of struggle. Communists have engaged and will engage in this tactic at times but always with regard to its impact on strategy—whether it helps or hinders bringing together the maximum of the necessary strategic forces.

• Lenin, in "Guerrilla Warfare," says it is not the job of the vanguard, of the Communist Party, to invent forms of struggle and organization or issues and demands, and to create schemes and plans for them. Instead, he argues, Marxists need to study which forms are developing and taking place and from that work out what comes next in tactics. Lenin speaks of "professors in their studies" and armchair revolutionaries creating schemes. These, he says, are useless systems.

Among the fetishes about forms of struggle is the denial that electoral activity is ever a useful form. For those anarchists who consider the state and government to be the source of all social evil, and who call for the end of the state—whether it is dominated by the capitalist class or by the working class and its allies—electoral activity diverts the struggle, breeds illusions, and perpetuates what has to be destroyed. Those who view the solution to society's problems as "one big union," the famous slogan of the old Industrial Workers of the World (IWW) or anarcho-syndicalists, also treat electoral activity as at best a diversion from the "real" path to revolution.

Many young people and others new to social struggle identify electoral politics with corruption, personal opportunism, and other diversions from genuine social change. Certainly there are office holders, candidates and large parts of national political parties that are controlled by big capital and in which many people are bought off and corrupted. Big money from the ultra-right and other sections of capital plays a huge role in elections and in the legislative and administrative functions of government.

But two processes impel ever greater electoral activity by the democratic and progressive forces. First, what government does or does not do has an ever-growing effect on the lives of working people. Over 1/3 of the total domestic product passes through government hands, and what the government does cannot be ignored. Second, the core forces for social progress have increasingly entered many forms of electoral struggle and pressure on government to achieve their needs and to prevent actions that harm them. They have had victories and partial victories, as well as some defeats. In presidential elections, 110 million people participate in a host of ways— voting, joining campaigns, petitions, resolutions, demonstrations, and other forms. The core forces of the working class (and its most organized sector, labor), the nationally oppressed, women, and youth have become highly involved in electoral struggle. Other forms of struggle remain very important—such as contract negotiations, strikes, demonstrations, direct action, etc.—but elections are now of vital importance in the number of participants, for what is at stake on issues, for the results, and for what is learned through participation.

The 2008 election of the Obama Administration and Congress changed the direction of the country on virtually all major issues from being increasingly reactionary and anti-social to moving in a more positive direction, at different speeds and to different extents on various issues. The strategic alliance of the core and other forces is largely formed in the course of electoral and legislative struggles. As in all struggles for progress, some illusions are clarified or destroyed, and some gain currency, but for the millions (as Lenin argued) it is in the course of such struggles that the basic outcome is the defeat of illusions and moving forward. Lenin is sometimes cited by those who oppose electoral-legislative activity. It is true that Lenin saw a limited role for it in the Stolypin Repression after the defeat of the Revolution of 1905. But he never ruled electoral work out in principle. In fact, as parliamentary and electoral struggle grew in Western Europe and the United States and showed more potential, in "Left-Wing Communism, An Infantile Disorder" [1920], Lenin criticized the "abstentionism on principle" tendency in the world movement. In his last years, Lenin argued for the importance of parliamentary struggle on many occasions. Here in the USA, the Communists emphasize electoral work when the core forces are active and through the instruments that they select, as a starting point. However, the objective is also to move toward a new people's party based on the core forces, led by the working class, and free of big capital domination.

• The united front or coalition style of work is vital to proper tactics. Marxists seek to build a working basis of unity based on where people are, not at maximum ideological levels. In a coalition, they seek give-and-take relations with other forces and a sharing of leadership responsibilities. Marxists oppose anyone seeking to capture leadership or conduct factionalism among the people's forces and organizations. Marxists seek openness to different views and adherence to agreed decisions. Characteristic of the ultra-left is persistent struggle for control and factionalism which prevents the broad unity of action necessary to mass movements and to achieve the agreed strategic goal. The ultras often approach such organizations and movements as though the sharper the internal struggle the better. Their aim in participating in demonstrations and other actions is to win people to their idea of revolutionary consciousness, not how to win the particular demand. They want to rope off small sections of the mass movement into their "revolutionary" corral or "hegemony" and continually add a small number to that corral. Sometimes demands are advanced that are considered impossible of attainment at that time or at all under capitalism, for the sake of advancing "consciousness." The result is not higher levels of consciousness but rather cynicism and distrust of the immature leftists who advance such propositions.

By the time the last person enters the "revolutionary" corral, though, the first sees the futility of isolation from mass struggles and leaves the corral.

The inexperienced left and the ultra-left often develop schematic forms of struggle and organization—a universal form of struggle everywhere, a single national center always. Some movements are so big as not yet to be ripe for a single center. Such a single center may not be necessary, and forcing it can cause disunity and other problems. Loose coordination and consultation may be the proper form to best serve strategy at a given moment. Will the all-people's front be a unitary organization or even a coalition of organizations or a single coordinating center? Not likely. Marxists always seek wider forms of unity but forcing it can produce the opposite and may not be necessary for effective functioning and unity. The same goes for the form or forms of a people's anti-monopoly coalition in the next stage of strategy. That is a tactical question of the form of organization which must grow out of the concrete course of development, not some preconceived format.

In a united front style of work, the aim is not to push the coalition as far to the left as possible. That is the aim if one is trying to corral a narrow sector off to the side. If the aim is to develop ever-wider unity in a progressive direction capable of winning the strategic objective of that stage, the bigger picture has to be taken into account and unity must be maintained while the whole advances in a progressive direction. There are always challenges to the existing level of unity, such as those reflecting anti-working class sentiments, racism and sexism. Overcoming these challenges requires raising the level of understanding on these issues and advancing the level of unity of the broad masses.

• Another principle guiding the proper selection of tactics concerns Lenin's often voiced warning to soberly assess the situation and especially its concrete relationship of forces. Wishful thinking will lead to wrong, unsuccessful or even harmful tactics. So will moral absolutes as a guide to tactics. Emotion, anger and a strong sense of working-class morality have their role and place, but they are not the basis for carefully estimating a situation and its existing balance of forces and studying the issues, demands, forms of struggle and organization that are actually developing in order to judge the most useful tactics at that point. Once the estimate of the situation has been made— the direction the struggle is headed, the current rela-

tionship of forces and the most useful tactics for the situation—
then conviction, fervor and knowledge of what is right and just can
play a positive role.

- In "'Left-wing' Communism," Lenin stresses the importance for
revolutionary strategy and tactics of seeking and developing all the
possible temporary, partial alliances of forces in order to move forward faster and further with less difficulty. We should not hesitate
because we know they are only temporary or partial alliances.

Strategy: The core forces for social progress

The working class

In Chapter 2, **The Political Economy of Capitalism** and Chapter
3, **Historical Materialism**, we discussed that the capitalist system
depends on the existence of the working class. It is the unpaid labor
of the working class that permits the capitalist class to realize surplus
value, profit, and to expand its capital. The working class is defined as
those who own no means of production or distribution and as a result
must sell their labor power to the capitalist owners. But there are other
definitions of class and of the working class, as well as denial of and
challenge to the Marxist definition. The universal Marxist definition
of class for all class societies was given by Lenin: "Classes are large
groups of people differing from each other by the place they occupy
in a historically determined system of social production, by their relation (in most cases fixed and formulated in law) to the means of production, by their role in the social organization of labor, and consequently by the dimensions of the share of social wealth of which they
dispose and the mode of acquiring it. Classes are groups of people one
of which can appropriate the labor of another owing to the different
places they occupy in a definite system of social economy." ("A Great
Beginning." July 1913, CW Vol. 29, p. 421) Capitalist media seldom
use the term "working class." They speak of the lower class, or the
poor, the middle class, and the upper class or the rich. The organized
working class is placed in the middle class. Non-Marxist sociologists
and other academics usually determine class on the basis of social status, income and/or wealth, or by whether a person considers himself
or herself to be upper class, middle class or lower class, or a combination of these factors. Much of this is done to obscure the most
meaningful concept of class, the Marxist one.

As a predictor of behavior over the long run, reflecting necessary interests of large groups of people, the Marxist view is the soundest. It reveals the contending nature of the interests of the working class and the capitalist class. And it reveals why the working class needs to fight the capitalist class to improve its living standards and avoid losing ground. It reveals why the working class needs to seek an end to the capitalist system to end its exploitation and relative and absolute impoverishment. It reveals that only the working class has the potential strength to end capitalism and the ability to build alliances to do so.

Class is not a matter of what class a person thinks he or she belongs to. Opinion polls of class membership have shifted back and forth radically over the years without any change in the objectively-existing class relations. It is not a matter of income though that goes along in large measure with the determining production relations. Many small business people and family farmers receive less income than do workers organized in mass production industries. But the small storekeepers are not in a position to combat big capital and lead the way to basic change. They do not have the conditions of highly interdependent labor and trade union organization. Nor does social status determine class interests and the trend of action and organization.

Why then is only the working class capable of leading the struggle for social progress and for socialism?

- First of all, because of its position in the system of social production in which it owns no means of production and distribution but must sell its ability to work to the capitalists who are the owners, in order to live. As a result, its unpaid labor time is the source of surplus value realized by the capitalists, and the resulting source of profit and capital. The system is dependent on the labor of the working class and so when workers strike or in other ways seek a greater share of the surplus value, they impact the whole economy and superstructure.

- The working class works together in substantial numbers and in highly interdependent, social conditions. Though the single work site tends to have fewer workers compared to the past, the company may be a transnational monopoly with work sites around the world. The workers at all these sites are in highly interdependent circumstances that lead to common action and organization, which gives them experience in organization and struggle and the possibility to realize their own potential strength.

* The working class in each developed capitalist country is the majority. In the U.S. it is about 150 million and growing. This represents great existing and potential strength to attract other class and social forces to its side on single issues and struggles and then in a general alliance, and it represents strength to combat the capitalist class in the economic, political and ideological arenas.

* The working class is composed of all nationalities, and is a majority of every nationality. Among the racially and nationally oppressed, the percentage that is working class is even greater. About 40 percent of the U.S. working class is nationally oppressed. Nearly the same percentage of women as of men is part of the working class, though not as high a percentage is organized as yet in unions. The working class also consists of skilled and unskilled, older and younger, organized and unorganized, employed, unemployed and partially employed, undocumented and documented immigrants and native-born, gay and straight. This social composition helps the working class develop its class consciousness and reject the divisive ideologies that benefit the capitalists, such as racism, male supremacy, sexism, anti-youth or anti-senior attitudes. It helps make possible good working relations with the racially and nationally oppressed as a whole across class lines, with women and youth as a whole across class lines, and others.

* These objective conditions of the working class give rise to the spontaneous development of trade union consciousness, initial levels of class consciousness and a receptivity to the full development of class consciousness which includes Marxism and socialism. These latter stages require the conscious involvement and help of a Communist Party, as we shall discuss in Chapter seven.

* The objective conditions of the working class also give rise to the recognition of the necessity for struggle for their interests in the economic arena—over wages, conditions and benefits through their unions, or to unionize, using a great variety of forms of struggle in union negotiations, including different kinds of work stoppages and actions. It means fighting for related demands in the legislative

arena and for a wider array of issues that affect workers' lives such as the struggles for peace, democracy, for full equality and against both racism and male supremacy. The economic struggle becomes also a political struggle both in the legislative arena and in the electoral arena. In the electoral arena, the working class struggles to elect candidates who are responsive to their demands by working through the major existing parties, by electing trade unionists, and by striving to build a party led by the working class which can challenge for electoral power and eventually for state power to build socialism.

• The working class is the only truly revolutionary class, as "The Manifesto" says, because the working class can only end its own exploitation by ending capitalism. Therefore, its interests are fundamentally incompatible with capitalism.

Trade union, class and socialist consciousness do not develop in a perfectly uniform, straight line. Some sections of the class develop faster and more consistently, with less slipping back on particular issues. Some sections lag behind because of a combination of objective conditions in their industry and subjective factors such as the success of the capitalists in dividing some of the workers or buying off or corrupting this or that trade union leader, or because there are not enough left-wing trade unionists in the given industry or local. It is also possible that some unions will play an advanced role on some issues but lag on others. When 250,000 trade union volunteers led the way in defeating the ultra-right majority in the House of Representatives and Senate in the 2006 elections, they achieved in life the leading role of the working class in the fight for progress. They led the way in changing the balance in Congress that impacted the whole country on all major issues and in the fight to defeat the Bush administration and the ultra-right as a whole. Yet that does not mean these trade union activists were necessarily the most advanced ideologically on all issues. Their leading role resulted from their objective position in society and being part of the front ranks of the organized workers, which gave them much more power and ability to change things.

It is for these reasons that Marxists assert the working class is the leading class for social progress and socialism, whether it already plays that role consistently on all issues or is in the process of assum-

ing that role. Since consciousness reflects but often lags the objectively existing conditions of social being, sooner or later under developed
capitalism, the working class assumes the leading role in the struggle
for social progress. That is a law of social development. But like all
laws of social development, it assumes the development of conscious
forces to fight for it to be realized in practice, and it recognizes the
capitalists will do all in their power to prevent it. Capitalists try to convince the workers that the interests of the capitalists ("their" capitalists) and "their" workers are identical, that the enemy is not the capitalists but rather other workers who differ in race or nationality, or sex,
or other characteristics, and who are then held responsible for workers' problems. The leading role of the working class is not a self-exe-
cuting law of social development but one that requires conscious
struggle, especially by the Communists and left forces.

The working class is growing with the entry of new strata, and with
the updating of the Marxist conception of the working class. At one
time only those who produced physical commodities were considered
workers. Service workers of all kinds were not included. Many of
these, such as office workers, were in a separate category of "employees" according to the Marxist economists and theoreticians of France
and the Soviet Union. Food industry and health care workers were
considered non-productive, if workers at all. Bank employees were
among the office employees. Teachers—and even more clearly, college teachers—were professionals and not workers. Scientific and
technological personnel were professionals. Airline pilots, co-pilots
and navigators were professionals, while flight attendants and ticket
issuers were considered service employees on the fringes of the working class.

Today, U.S. Marxists consider all of these categories and more to be
part of the various strata that make up the working class. Among those
considered professional workers, there are administrators who are
really part of management. These include college department heads,
public school principals and partners in a law firm who have many
lawyers and paralegals working for them on weekly or hourly salary.
These managerial or semi-managerial jobs are not part of the working
class. There are borderline situations that are not very significant for
practical purposes since they do not involve large numbers or have
clear-cut interests one way or the other. By theoretical definition, in all

the working class jobs—whether in production or circulation, office work, government jobs or other service jobs—necessary labor is performed so that either production of commodities takes place or the non-productive labor enables another part of the capitalist class to share in the surplus value created in the sphere of production of material or non-material commodities.

Advances in the forces of production, enlargement of the sphere of circulation of commodities as compared to the sphere of commodity production, enlargement of the sphere of non-material commodities production such as information—are all enlarging the working class and proletarianizing new sectors of the population on whose useful but unpaid labor power capitalists' profits depend. Globalization is further enlarging the world working classes.

Thus the working class is growing rapidly, and as Marx predicted, sectors formerly in the middle strata have become workers and are being proletarianized. The working class is becoming more diverse internally even while all of its members become more proletarianized and have more reason to struggle together for better wages, conditions and benefits. There is, at least temporarily, an upper strata of the working class, especially among the most skilled scientific and technological sections. They are doing better than the bulk of the working class, but even this strata suffers from insecurity as even such skilled jobs can quickly be moved overseas. Or, some good technical jobs disappear with rapid changes in technology, which replace workers.

The internationalization of economic life under capitalism, dominated by the growth of the transnational monopolies (globalization and financialization), is having a profound effect on the lives of working people in the U.S. No longer can the bulk of the working class spend a lifetime in the same occupation and possibly working for the same company. No longer can young people grow up expecting to follow in the footsteps of their parents as to occupation and industry. Studies show that during a lifetime, the average person will have to find a new occupation four or five times. Often the succeeding occupations will be unorganized and lower paying. The speed with which companies close down and/or move out of the country has grown. And ever new occupations are moved out of the country. Manufacturing continues to decline and niche manufacturing replaces giant mass production. Within the U.S., transportation, pharmaceuticals and many other industries decline in domestic employment even though they expand in worldwide employment and may remain headquartered in the U.S. or offshore.

The leading capitalists in the U.S. and the other most developed capitalist countries are now encouraging large temporary immigration of workers and/or favor a large semi-legal immigrant workforce who do not have full rights and whose labor does not cost as much. Large companies are forcing cuts in their health care and pension costs and seeking to shift these expenses to the workers themselves and/or to public funds, while corporate taxes are minimized. Taken together these are all substantial pressures on a majority of the working class to accept stagnant or declining wages. For the poorest sections of the working class, in which the nationally oppressed are very heavily represented, a steady decline in real wages is typical. The squeeze on working-class living standards also arises from rising costs for food, housing, medical care, transportation and education, while taxes for these sections rise, often in the form of fees and increased rents to cover property taxes.

In mid-2008 a U.S.-initiated world financial and economic crisis broke out. Its impact on the working class and all working people is hard to overstate. The most severe impact is on the racially and nationally oppressed and youth. At this writing, the impact on workers is only now emerging and is expected to get much worse. It is also expected to last much longer than any other recession since World War II. Ten million workers are already unemployed in the U.S. Four million are in the process of losing their homes. Additional millions are losing their health care and/or pensions. State and city services of important benefit to workers are being cut back drastically because of budget shortfalls. The election of the Barack Obama ticket and increase in the Democratic majority in Congress were powered in the working class to the economic crisis.

As such a squeeze grows, the working class' level of activity and consciousness, and especially that of the organized labor movement, grows in the form of ever-higher levels of electoral activity marked by leftward shifts, as well as increasing efforts to organize the unorganized. Efforts to find forms of international labor solidarity grow rapidly, including merger of unions across international boundaries.

The core forces and special oppression and exploitation

Big sections of the working class not only face the problems of the whole working class but also additional special oppression and exploitation. Often they are paid lower wages for the same work or for work of comparable value. That means they are paid below the value of their labor power and extra surplus value or super profits are realized from this special oppression and exploitation. Special oppression applies widely to the racially and nationally oppressed and also applies to women and often to youth. "Last hired and first fired" still applies to a considerable extent despite anti-discrimination laws. Workers also experience being passed over for promotion. There are also forms of special oppression that apply to these workers and to the middle strata and even to the small section of these categories who are capitalists. These include violence on the street and from the police, inferior conditions in every aspect of life, or a failure to meet their special needs. The corporate-owned media and culture are full of insults and belittlement and forms that encourage violence against them. Many of these conditions directly produce extra money for big capital, while much is part of the effort to divide working people who could and should be allies, to safeguard extra profits for the dominant capitalist circles.

It is the capitalist class that gains from this special oppression and exploitation. The working class, as a class, does not gain, but actually loses when it is divided internally, or non-working class sections of the specially oppressed are pitted against the working class in a misunderstanding of self-interest. When the impact of racism causes division among workers, white workers are also worse off. It should be noted that some white workers labor in industries where they are paid less than African American workers in industries with stronger unions or other particular circumstances. It is also true that a white worker may obtain a job that is refused to an equally qualified African American worker. The individual white worker benefits from such discrimination. At the same time, it is against his or her class interest, as it weakens the unity of the class as a whole and therefore, what the class can win in combat with capital.

The basis exists for the specially oppressed as a whole—not only their working class sector—to become allies of the working class as a whole against the capitalist class.

The racially and nationally oppressed

Special oppression and exploitation exists for those people singled out and identified on the basis of their nationality and physical appearance as darker peoples. These include African Americans, Afro-Caribbeans, Africans; Mexican Americans, Puerto Ricans, Dominicans and other Latinos; Native Americans; Chinese, Filipinos, Japanese and others from East Asia and the Pacific Islands; Indians, Pakistanis and others from South Asia; Palestinians, Lebanese, Egyptians, Iraqis and other Arab peoples, Iranians and other peoples of Central Asia. Most are darker are darker in color or otherwise easily identifiable and come from poor countries. Many are undocumented, especially from Mexico, Latin America, China and South Asia. All experience special, additional oppression and exploitation beyond that normally experienced by the working class as a whole. And those who are not working-class experience special forms of oppression visited on these peoples as a whole.

Some of this history was discussed in Chapter 3, **Historical Materialism**, about forms of human community. Human community was discussed as a most important aspect of each socioeconomic formation, closely related to but not actually a part of either the base or superstructure of society. We then discussed human community as it had and was still developing in the United States. Here we shall single out several peoples in the U.S. from the standpoint of their history, and present conditions and role in the development of the alliance for advance of the working class and the core forces for progress.

African Americans

The role of slavery, Jim Crow and the Civil Rights revolution have already received attention in previous chapters. A very small section of the African American people have become capitalists and are doing better, but even they are subject to racist violence and police brutality and to the cultural content in the media that demeans African Americans. The vast majority of African Americans are part of the working class and of its poorer half. Billions of dollars are reaped each year by the capitalists as a result of paying African American workers less for the same work or work of comparable value. Capitalists also reap extra profit from the labor of African Americans and other specially oppressed peoples by compelling more overtime work, night-shift work without premium pay, less safety equipment, and so on. When the labor movement is weakened by internal divisions fostered by the ruling class, the capitalists also succeed in paying white workers below the value of their labor power due to the North-South differential which, though less, still continues.

In every aspect of life—housing, schools, health care, community facilities and on the job—the general rule is that African American workers in comparable work experience worse conditions than white workers. Conditions are getting worse for all workers, but especially for African American and other specially oppressed workers. The Black population of New York and many other cities is declining because rising housing and other costs are driving them out in search of cheaper areas to live. African Americans, and especially the youth, experience increased targeting by the police. The prison population, disproportionately African American, has grown rapidly. The effort by the ultra-right to disfranchise African Americans, Latinos and Native Americans, including on Election Day, has increased considerably. It is a central question of electoral struggle in the fight for progress.

At the same time, the role of African Americans in the labor movement, including that of the Coalition of Black Trade Unionists, has grown greatly. African Americans consistently vote between 85 and 95% against the far right and for more liberal and progressive candidates. The Congressional Black Caucus now has over 40 members and plays a big role in conjunction with the labor movement, the Congressional Progressive Caucus and peace caucus. There is no area of U.S. life in which the issue of full real equality for the African American people and the fight against racism aimed at them does not play a key role in deciding the direction of the country as a whole. In all areas of the struggle for peace, democracy and progress, the fight for equality and the role of the African American people is key in determining the outcome. The campaign and the election of Barack Obama as the first African American president demonstrates the role of the fight for equality and against racism. Reaction recognizes that key role and consistently fights against full equality and spreads racism. The progressive forces, starting with labor, are coming to recognize it and to build the core alliance of labor, the African American people, other key oppressed people such as the Mexican American and all Latino peoples, women and youth.

Mexican Americans, Puerto Ricans and other Latinos

Mexican Americans, Puerto Ricans, Dominicans and many other Latino nationalities are well represented in nearly every area of the U.S. Some history of the largest nationalities and the nationality development processes is discussed in Chapter 3, **Historical Materialism**, under Human Communities. Included is how these peoples became part of the nationally oppressed within the U.S. They are among the most working-class of all the peoples that make up the U.S. nation. Latinos, taken together, have become the most numerous nationality category, with Mexican Americans the single most populous nationality group after African Americans. They too suffer second-class conditions everywhere and are a source of super-profits. Such special oppression is also used as an instrument to divide the working class as a whole and therefore to reduce the wages of white workers as well. A large proportion of the Latino population are undocumented workers who do not have equal rights with other workers and as a result have to take the lowest paying jobs and live in the shadows, subject to government raids, deportation and the breaking up of families.

Crossing the border in search of a decent livelihood and reunification of families, the undocumented have to risk their lives as the U.S. government and racist vigilante organizations increase the physical risks. Latinos—documented, native-born and undocumented—also face suppression of the Spanish language, cultural deprivation and media insults. Thus the conditions of life and interests of this section of the population and their fight-back on many fronts have also become central to both the unity of the working class and to alliance with the other core forces in the fight for democracy and progress. Once again the ultra-right is making a growing effort to keep the Latino vote down, as this vote is also overwhelmingly against them and on the side of the working class as a whole and the African American people.

The forms of oppression and the needs of each Latino nationality have both similarities and particular features. The Puerto Rican people living in the U.S. proper are U.S. citizens but they are also among the poorest sections of the population and among the most working-class, with one of the highest rates of union organization. The 4 million Puerto Ricans living in Puerto Rico inhabit one of the last colonies in the world, according to the United Nations, and suffer those forms of oppression. They have a right to self-determination by any means they choose, including independence, which is most likely what they would choose in a really democratic plebiscite. While the unsatisfactory Commonwealth status continues, the ultra-right in the U.S. is still attempting to impose statehood on the people of Puerto Rico.

Native Americans and other indigenous peoples

The mainland U.S. was taken by force from the Native Americans who now number about 5 million. Less than half live on reservations controlled by the Indian Bureau, which often acts to repress the people while it protects capitalist profits. Native Americans not on the reservations are overwhelmingly working-class. Many are unemployed. The Hawaiian Islands were also taken by force, while Alaska, home to indigenous Aleuts and others, was bought from Russia. All of these peoples suffer some of the highest poverty levels in our country. Casinos are an insecure and inadequate source of reservation livelihood and even they do not exist in most places. Native Americans must be given control of the Indian Bureau. Again the ultra-right seeks to take away their right to vote because Native Americans are increasingly allying themselves with the other racially and nationally oppressed and with labor and the whole working class.

Asians and Pacific Islanders

Asians and Pacific Islanders are the third largest nationally oppressed grouping. In Chapter 3, Historical Materialism, the section on Human Communities provides some discussion of their history and their relationship to the national question in the U.S. The earliest Asians were brought to the U.S. in semi-bondage—Chinese to build railroads and engage in metal mining, Filipinos and others to work in the fields of Hawaii and California. Together with Mexicans, Chinese are the fastest growing group of undocumented workers. The most working-class of the nationally oppressed from Asia are the Chinese, Filipinos, Pakistanis and Bangladeshis. There are also sizable Indian and Japanese populations in the U.S., including Japanese families who suffered internment in concentration camps during World War II and continue to demand adequate reparations for that violation of human rights. In addition to the forms of extra exploitation and oppression and other forms of racism and national oppression which cut across class lines, there are also issues of language, culture, and immigration and lack of documentation. While there are differences among the various nationalities, a majority now opposes the ultra-right and is allying itself with the other racially and nationally oppressed and with the working class and labor as a whole as part of the core forces for social progress.

Arab and other Islamic Asian peoples

About 6 million Arabs from Palestine, Lebanon, Iraq, Egypt and other countries live in the U.S. There are also millions of Muslims from Iran, Afghanistan, Pakistan, Bangladesh, Indonesia and other countries. Besides the conditions faced by other racially and national-ly oppressed peoples, they face deprivation of democratic rights, deportation, police profiling and false imprisonment at a very high level under the ultra-right-engineered "anti-terrorism" campaign. In the 2006 elections, those who could vote for the first time joined the anti-ultra-right majority in alliance with the other nationally oppressed.

The Jewish people and anti-Semitism

From the time of major migration from Eastern Europe at the end of the 19th century, the Jews living in ghettoes of big cities were among the specially oppressed peoples. Lenin had characterized their oppression as national, though in religious garb. But soon after World War II, the bulk of the Jewish population achieved economic equality with the dominant population and did not suffer the kind of daily spe-cial oppression experienced by other specially oppressed peoples. However, anti-Semitism still is a useful tool of the ultra-right. Now it takes the form of claims that the Jews own all the wealth and control the government. Anti-Semitism is still expressed in violence and van-dalism against synagogues, and in some areas against homes and Jewish individuals. The ultra-right assault on the separation of church and state is of deep concern to Jews, whose history includes periods of extreme persecution and forced conversion to Christianity.

While most Jews are workers, they are usually white collar work-ers. Jews are represented among the wealthy and big capitalists but are far from the dominant national group among big capital. While a sec-tion, especially of better-off Jews, has supported the Israeli government's policies of occupation and repression against the Palestinians, most favor a just, two-state solution, an end to occupation and settlements, return to the 1967 borders, Jerusalem as capital of both states and negotiation of the refugee issue. Because of their history of oppression and their having been part of the New Deal coalition, the Jewish people vote overwhelmingly against the ultra-right and together with the core forces for democracy and social progress and for peace. The Jewish vote went 78% for Barack Obama.

Women

As Engels demonstrated in "The Origin of the Family, Private Property and the State" (1884), special oppression of women began when the development of the forces of production led to private property in the means of production and a class-divided society. But the forms of oppression underwent some changes with each new socioeconomic formation, and while often using the forms of oppression from prior societies, the purposes of special oppression and exploitation underwent changes. Now nearly as great a percentage of women as men are in the workforce, but their average pay remains substantially lower, which means women are often paid below the value of their labor power for equal work or work of comparable value and the capitalists realize extra surplus value and super profits. Where the disparity in wages also means divisions in the working class, and therefore weakness in the struggle against the boss, it results in less pay for men as well.

Women also bear the unequal burden of care and concern for the family in domestic labor and childcare. The issues of day care, schools and education, health care and housing, all weigh more heavily on women. Women also suffer from physical violence both in the home and outside, and from treatment widely in society as sexual objects, out of which the capitalists realize additional billions in profit. The culture and media remain full of stereotypes and degradation of women. Women's reproductive rights are under severe attack in state legislatures, the courts and Congress. The legal cornerstone of those rights, Roe v. Wade, is in serious danger. Affirmative action programs for women, as well as for the nationally oppressed, have been rolled back and also are in serious danger.

Every section of women faces special burdens. Single mothers, among whom are an especially high proportion of racially and nationally oppressed women, are among the most poverty-stricken sections of the population.

A glass ceiling still exists even for the most highly educated and skilled women, who have been able to achieve some professional and administrative status.

Women are active in the labor movement. They are much more active than men in all community struggles, and they are more numerous and active in the peace movement. There is also a voting gap between women and men, with women voting significantly more against the ultra-right and at the side of the working class, labor, the racially and nationally oppressed and youth, as part of the core forces for social progress. The alliance of women with the working class and other core forces flows from a commonality of interests and from overlapping populations. Women are now equally of the working class as men and somewhat more women than men are nationally and racially oppressed. A large sector of young women face a host of special problems.

Youth

Under capitalism, youth also face special oppression and exploitation. Youth is a biological and psychological category applying to the transition period between childhood and adulthood, experienced under all socioeconomic formations. Youth have special needs on the path to adulthood. Under capitalism, most youth suffer special social oppression and exploitation. Like all age categories, youth have a class position, class origin (family class position), class outlook or ideology. But among youth, class position and class outlook are still developing and not yet fixed.

Among the special needs of youth are an adequate and affordable education, democratic in content and including knowledge about life and preparation for employment. Education should be free at least from pre-school through undergraduate college. Youth require job training and specific education so they can get and keep a job and earn a living. For many, starting a family is related to acquiring stable employment. Youth need world peace so they do not become cannon-fodder in capitalism's wars. They need a democratic education in school and in society so that racism is rejected and they can better live with all peoples. Youth need recreation, sports and cultural outlets so they can develop their special talents and interests, which in turn enriches the culture of their communities.

But capitalists do not want to be taxed, or spend their profits, on such things. They want youth for their international adventures and wars. They want youth as cheap labor to undermine trade union standards. Two-tier wage systems and over-long probation periods, substandard wage "apprenticeship" periods and low minimum wages are all methods of achieving wages below value, and the resulting extra surplus value and super profits. So too is a long-term army of unemployed youth, especially among youth who are also racially and nationally oppressed and/or young women—a result of capitalism today. The ultra-right also seeks to keep down the youth vote. Politically the capitalists seek to win the young generation to the side of capitalism in general but particularly to the side of reaction.

Youth usually have little opportunity to learn about the progressive history of the U.S., the role of the labor movement, of the national freedom and equality movements of the racially and nationally oppressed, of the women's equality movement or the left wing and the Communists. To know the central lessons of the American Revolution, of the Civil War and Reconstruction, of the organization of the mass production industries and the New Deal, of the Civil Rights revolution, of peace and international solidarity, is to rebuff the advances of reaction in trying to win the young generation. Such knowledge helps win the young generation to the side of the working class and labor as a whole, and to the side of the other core forces, the nationally oppressed and women. The youth are moving in that direction. They are an important part of labor struggles, struggles for full quality and against racism and a major part of the peace movement. Youth are especially sensitive to the need to fight for a livable, sustainable environment. They are voting overwhelmingly against the increasingly part of the core forces for social progress.

There are several intertwined reasons why all sections of the population who suffer special oppression and exploitation are drawn together with one another and with the working class as a whole. The source of the special oppression in each case is what benefits the capitalist class, and particularly its most reactionary sectors. These include the financial benefits of extra surplus value and super profits, and the political benefits for the right reaped from divisions fostered among these natural allies. They are natural allies because the forms of special oppression and exploitation are similar and often intertwined. They are natural allies because the enemy, the cause of the special problems, is identical or nearly so. They are natural allies because there is such a big overlap in populations. The working class today is by a substantial majority also composed of the specially oppressed, of women, the racially and nationally oppressed, and youth. There can be no unity of the working class without taking into account the special demands of the specially oppressed necessary to win their full, real equality and with that, higher standards for the whole working class.

6 Marxist Methodology: Tool of Struggle

❖ The working class standpoint or outlook
❖ Interconnection and interpenetration
❖ Approach all questions historically
❖ Dialectical materialism
❖ Materialism
❖ Dialectics and its laws
❖ Dialectical categories: The lesser laws of dialectics
❖ Appearance and essence
❖ The universal, the general and the particular
❖ Necessity and chance (or accident)
❖ Cause and effect
❖ Form and content
❖ Theory as methodology
❖ Key link in the chain

All activity for social progress and socialism, whether political, organizational or ideological, requires a methodology to succeed. Methodology embraces all the laws, theories and principles of social development, the physical and natural sciences and of thought that make possible assessing change and the existing situation and determining how to respond. Methodology has a class aspect to it, as we shall see. The methodology which most corresponds to the interests of the working class is Marxist methodology. There also is at least one methodology that corresponds to the interests of the capitalist class, and methodology that corresponds to the interests of the middle strata.

If one is studying developments in the political economy of capitalism, methodology is needed to analyze objective processes in the economy. Studying how new technology affects the relations of production, property relations and the superstructure requires methodology. Studying whether the anti-ultra-right strategic stage of struggle has been completed and the anti-monopoly strategic stage has been reached requires methodology. Figuring out what are the best, most appropriate tactics to complete the anti-ultra-right strategic stage

155

requires methodology. Assessing the stage that has been reached in a shop or neighborhood struggle and deciding the central demand and the best forms of organization and struggle to fight for it requires methodology. If the task is how to build a union, a YCL chapter, a Communist Party club, methodology is needed. To decide how to go from where we are all the way to socialism requires methodology. To think like a Marxist requires a grasp of Marxist methodology.

What are the guides for Marxist methodology?
The working class standpoint or outlook

Marxist methodology approaches all questions from the standpoint of the real interests of the working class. That means asking yourself what is in the interests of the working class in every situation. What should I do to act in the interests of the working class in the given situation? What does having a working-class outlook mean in the given situation? The reason for this is that what is actually in the long-term interests of the working class as a whole is also in the interests of humanity, social progress and socialism. (See Chapters 2 and 3.)

Sometimes what is in the interests of the working class is obvious. But sometimes it is not so simple. The capitalist class has learned how to pit one section of the working class against another and their short-term interests against their long-term interests. In contract negotiations, the company will offer some gain or will not fight for a particular give-back, if the workers as a whole accept a two-tier wage system in which new hires get paid at a lower rate for the same work done by those with higher seniority. When workers reject such a proposal, they understand what is in the interests of all the workers, not just some. But settling a contract involves an estimate of the balance of forces. Can or can't the company take a strike? Are the workers ready to strike if they do not win certain terms in a contract? Will the union emerge stronger or weaker from a strike? There are periods in which nearly all unions are winning advances in contracts and periods in which nearly all are losing ground. Which advances are more important for all the workers in the long run? Which concessions are least harmful to all the workers in the long run? To reach sound conclusions, these questions must be studied on the basis of the interests of all the workers involved and their interests over the long run. What is in the interests of the working class may take very careful study to understand, and occasionally even then the answer may not be clear and trial and error may be needed.

The issue to be decided may directly concern the economic interests of the working class such as a contract, or it may be less direct. The capitalists sometimes offer a cut in taxes, mainly for the wealthy and corporations, but with some cuts for working people, to get them to buy into the proposal. They do not mention at the time what government spending will be cut to pay for the reduced taxes. Again, this requires studying and weighing gains and losses for the whole working class in the long run, and gains and losses for the capitalists.

With regard to immigration, the capitalist class, particularly its most reactionary sector, includes tradeoffs in the legislation it supports. On the one hand the reactionary proposal concedes a path to citizenship for millions of undocumented working people (though a long, difficult one) which is on the whole desirable from a working-class point of view. But this is often coupled with a guest worker provision which is against the interests of all workers, and anti-human provisions with regard to border "security." This latter is also clearly anti-working class. What are the realistic alternatives? Are we better off with no new legislation until the relationship of forces is changed in the Congress and White House? What is in the interests of the working class as a whole in the long run in this situation? With the defeat of the ultra-right in the 2008 national elections, a significantly better bill is quite possible, even one without any major negative features. But in the meantime, increased raids against the undocumented may take place. Thus determining the class interests is sometimes difficult and requires being sure to consider all sides of an issue and all interconnections. That brings us to a second principle of Marxist methodology.

Interconnection and interpenetration

To conclude what attitude to take on a particular issue, what is in the interests of the working class, and what tactics to pursue in achieving those interests, everything must be examined not in isolation but in all of its interconnections. What is the overall balance of forces that influences the particular question? If we are expecting the ultra-right to lose control of the executive and legislative organs of government, how will that influence the question at hand? Will a given national relationship of forces be upheld in the local situation, surpassed, or not be upheld locally? These are important questions determining the prospects in a concrete struggle and what strategy and tactics to pursue in the interests of the working class.

Approach all questions historically

Every issue and struggle has a history. The past is part of that. So are the present and the possibilities for the future. Marxists examine questions in their development, their process of change. To know about something's antecedents is to know something that may well influence the outcome of the given struggle. To know about the history of racism in the U.S. is to understand why it is such a major, persistent, tough struggle. It is also to know more clearly who the enemy is, why that is the enemy, who stands on the side of progress and the interests of the working class as a whole and who can be won to the fight for progress. Knowing accurately what level the struggle has reached in the present is also very important. Some people think the struggle for full equality is nearly won, and that organized, conscious opposition no longer exists. In this view, things are getting better. The inferior conditions of life of the African American and other peoples are substantially less. Leave things alone, and the remaining problems will disappear with time.

But while things may be somewhat better for a small segment of the African American people who have become capitalists and perhaps some in the top levels of the middle strata and working class, living standards have declined for the great bulk of the African American people who are of the working class, and second-class citizenship continues. The bottom half of wage earners have lost 15 % of real income in the last 20 years and a very high percentage of these workers are African Americans or other racially and nationally oppressed people. The African American population of New York, Atlanta, Boston, Washington D.C., Cleveland, San Francisco and many other cities is declining because the cost of living—and especially housing—has gone up substantially, their wages have not, and jobs have disappeared.

Knowing accurately what stage developments have reached is part of viewing things historically. Where will they go next? There are two possibilities. Left alone, they will continue in the same direction and will get worse. If the progressive and democratic forces recognize what is going on and unite on the basis of a concrete program of compensatory treatment, affirmative action and unity of the nationally oppressed with the whole of labor and the other core social forces, the direction can be changed with continued solid effort. If it is not changed, all working people will suffer severely, including from internal divisions. An accurate historical approach is necessary to the struggle for progress. To ignore the past, out of which today's conditions developed, is to attribute the present to unforeseeable, accidental events, to deny dialectical materialism, and to know little of what currently exists and of possibilities for further development.

Dialectical materialism
Materialism

The capitalist propagandists and ideologists try to convince the working class and all working people that all complaints against capitalism are figments of our imagination. There are no great social ills—or they have no connection with capitalism. Phil Gramm, former senator from Texas and economic advisor to the ultra-right, proclaims complaints about the economy are not based on reality but rather are expressions of "whiners."

For years we were told cigarette smoking was perfectly healthy. There is no such thing as global warming. Evolution is only a theory, no more valid than the theories of creationism or intelligent design. There is no such thing as objective, scientific truth. A multitude of evidence from archeology, geology, biology, physics and chemistry, which forms the basis for all kinds of daily production and activity, is dismissed as speculative theory. Everything is a matter of subjective opinion, of each individual's sense perceptions and tastes. One person's opinion is as good as another's. If the advertising is frequent enough and clever enough, you can get anybody to believe anything. Truth will not out. You can fool everybody as long as you want, especially if you have enough money to put your message across. These are all expressions of what used to be known to philosophers as "idealism." It began with the proposition that the mind was dominant and created the universe, that there is no objective reality independent of our concepts and sense perceptions.

The early materialists and Marx, Engels and Lenin argued that there was an objective reality, independent of any mind, and it developed according to laws inherent in it. Being was primary and consciousness secondary, or reflected it. All of objective reality was knowable even though at any point it might not yet be known at all or not known fully. In his theory of knowledge, Lenin argued that truth was both absolute and relative. It was absolute in that it reflected a reality existing independent of our minds. But it was relative in that we were always learning more about particular objects, processes and reality in general, getting closer to but never gaining complete knowledge of the universe outside us. The test of reliable, accurate, truthful knowledge is practice in its many forms of testing. Therefore, practice is the test of theory and enables us to establish what is true in the sense in which Lenin discussed it.

The capitalist class is constantly interested in either hiding the truth or twisting it to blame others and cover up for itself and its system. That is why much of what the capitalists say and do is based on idealism and they reject materialism, which seeks the truth and helps secure the truth. Abraham Lincoln's aphorism, "You can fool some of the people all of the time and all of the people some of the time, but you cannot fool all of the people all of the time," holds true and places him among the materialists. Despite all the propaganda to hide social evils and their causes, life's experiences—especially when helped by the conscious Marxists using Marxist tools—make the truth a possession the masses can act upon. One can tell the worker everything is fine and anybody can become a rich capitalist but that is not his or her experience or that of fellow workers. The real world does exist and we can know it. Knowing it, we can help change it by collective struggle, especially when guided by Marxism.

Dialectics and its laws

Dialectics explains change, and especially how and why one object, process or phenomenon develops into another. Building on prior philosophers, Marx, Engels and Lenin explained what everyone could observe, not only past and present development of objects, processes or phenomena out of prior ones but also what could be expected to develop anew. Repetitive motion occurs when a tire turns while a car is driven, or when speedup occurs every day on a production line. Mechanical motion occurs when a stick hits a ball. But there is also developmental or dialectical motion. As the tire revolves on the car wheel, it wears out to the point where it undergoes a qualitative, developmental change, and can no longer function as a tire for car locomotion. On the factory floor, the workers become increasingly fed up with the speedup as they suffer with it every day. The result is a slow-down, or a qualitative change ending the repetitive activity. A new qualitative state develops out of a previous, different state.

After study and theorizing, Marx, Engels and Lenin concluded that development in nature, society and thought took place the same way, by common, universal laws of development. Knowing that was of great practical use as Marxist methodology.

How does development from one qualitative state to another take place? The three most general, universal laws of development, of dialectics are:

- Quantitative buildup to a certain point where a qualitative leap takes place; those quantitative changes have brought about a change in the qualitative character of the object, process or phenomenon. The qualitative change then leads to new quantitative changes. The qualitative change can take place in a single, sharp leap or in slower stages. When water is heated, causing slow quantitative changes in its temperature, and reaches 100 degrees centigrade, it takes a qualitative leap to a different quality, steam. When its temperature is lowered to 0 degrees centigrade the "leap" is to ice, a different quality.

  The British Revolution from feudalism to capitalism was a qualitative change but it took hundreds of years and a number of revolutionary episodes to complete. The U.S. Civil War was a bourgeois democratic revolution in the South but was cut short by the defeat of Reconstruction. A new qualitative state was not fully completed even when Jim Crow was overthrown by the Civil Rights Revolution of the 1960s led by Rev. Dr. Martin Luther King, Jr. The form in which development takes place requires quantitative changes leading to a qualitative change. But what is the content of the quantitative change that determines what the new dominant qualities will be?

- Unity and struggle of opposites. Internal to all objects, processes and phenomena is a unity and struggle of opposites. One aspect of the opposites consists of the qualities which determine what the object currently is. It is itself a more or less stable unity of opposites of the existing, dominant unity or entity. It is relatively stable to produce the kind of object that exists to begin with. But there is also a main aspect that is its opposite. This aspect grows quantitatively to the point where it becomes the dominant aspect. As it grows quantitatively, it is struggling to overcome what presently determines the dominant quality of the object.

When the contending opposite reaches the point where it becomes dominant, the old struggle of opposites is replaced by a new struggle of opposites. Now the struggle between the old dominant qualities of existence that are being replaced by the main possibility of new qualities of existence. This is the internal content of the change of quantity leading to a change in quality. Gradually the contending opposite gets stronger and leads to a change in quality in which it becomes dominant. In social development from one socioeconomic system to another, the abstracted process is the same as a seed developing into a plant, and then into a flower.

Under feudalism, the rising capitalist class is one of the contending classes or opposites growing in strength compared to the lords who are the dominant opposite that determines the character of feudalism. When the quantitatively strengthening capitalist class reaches the point of dominance, a qualitative change is reached and capitalism replaces feudalism. But the new unity of opposites in one location is never a 100% copy of what took place or is taking place elsewhere.

External influences also produce changes that are secondary to the internal primary contradiction. And within each opposite of the unity of opposites are internal contradictions that can change the main opposites to some extent so that the new unity of opposites with a new dominant aspect will have secondary features that are not a simple repetition in all respects but are accidental in their particular expression. No two capitalist countries are exactly alike even in all their main socioeconomic qualities. And yet they are capitalist countries. No two plants are exactly alike as they develop from seed through their main characteristics as plants, though they are the same kind of plant.

• The negation of the negation. This law explains why the previous processes do not result in a repetitive circle when continued. When the quantitative changes reach a qualitative turning point, in philosophical language that is the first time an opposite overcomes the previously dominant opposite and that constitutes the first "negation." When that negation leads to new quantitative growth until a new opposite becomes dominant with new qualities, why do the original opposite and dominant qualities not reappear? That would be a cyclical repetition.

But Engels explained that the second negation, or "the negation of the negation" meant continuing in an upward, progressive spiral instead. That is because the second negation carries forward with it anything from the previous negation that is still useful under the new conditions. Every new socioeconomic formation continues to employ means of production that are still useful. Materials, machinery, technology and techniques continue to be used and developed under the qualitatively new relations of production. Other aspects of the prior society or negation may prove useful in the new society, which is a "negation of the negation."

What is the practical use of these laws in social struggle? How do they serve Marxist methodology in the class struggle? It is very important to know when a qualitative turning point has taken place and when it has not yet been reached. Therefore, it is necessary constantly to look for it.

The 2006 elections began a qualitative turning point, the defeat of the ultra-right section of transnational monopolies in their dominance of all branches of government. Many changes in the atmosphere in the U.S. followed from this, but the qualitative change had not yet been completed. The Executive Branch and the Supreme Court still remained in their hands. Both those conclusions from an examination of qualitative change were of great importance in working out strategy and tactics. The 2008 elections produced a further qualitative change. The ultra-right lost control of the Executive and Congressional Branches, and in the main had been defeated. But the anti-monopoly stage of struggle had not been entered as a whole. Rather a transitional phase between the two stages had been entered, necessary to reach the anti-monopoly stage by a general growing over from one into the other. An accurate assessment of these qualitative changes was of great importance to develop sound strategy and tactics.

Every struggle has such turning points. It is very important to recognize them when they take place. To miss a qualitative turning point will result in underestimating new possibilities of struggle. To "see" a qualitative turn when it has not taken place, leads to proposing strategy and tactics that are ahead of development.

To know correctly the main characteristics of the two major contending opposites is to understand what is the possible content of the coming resolution of the contending opposites, and what possible qualities can emerge from the new struggle of opposites. Asking these questions and being clear on the answers is very important to strategy and tactics. If the contending opposites and the possible new qualitative state are not clear, it is not a good idea to mechanically force an answer into such an abstract universal law. It is better to use more concrete judgments and trial and error. Mistakes have been made through pursuing rigid schemes as to what are the thesis, the antithesis and the synthesis.

Dialectical categories or lesser laws of dialectics

Dialectical categories are lesser laws of dialectics, not as important as the first three. But they are universal laws. They exist in all objective reality. Each is a statement that if A exists, B will exist. Most of them have great practical significance for guiding theoretical work, strategy and tactics.

- **Appearance and essence.** Everything has an outward appearance which does not completely reveal its essential character. Marx famously remarked that if we could know everything from its appearance, we would not need science. Marxists need to avoid accepting appearance as completing our knowledge and constituting the essence of something. The capitalist class often uses appearance to hide the real essence. The appearance of the ultra-right legislation on immigration is that its backers want to keep "illegal" immigrants out. The reality or essence is they want to spread chauvinism and racism to divide the working class, using these working people as a scapegoat for loss of jobs. The aim is also to win elections. They also want to use the legislation as a cover to pass a guest worker program. This would bring in large numbers of workers who face second-class conditions and protections, causing them to suffer and undermining the conditions of the entire working class. Everything, both desirable and undesirable, has both an appearance and an essence.

- **The universal, the general and the particular.** All objects, processes and phenomena have aspects that are universal or general, but also, at the same time, particular. The class struggle is a universal feature of capitalism. But each of its expressions has both universal qualities and is particular, never a 100% copy of any previous expression. It is harmful to overlook the particular features, which leads to mechanical applications, isolation and defeat, or to overlook the universal and general features which show us how to connect a particular episode with workers elsewhere. In the construction of socialism, the particular features of each country were severely underestimated and the Soviet Union was copied mechanically. This was an important factor in the defeat of socialism in Eastern Europe. But to overlook the universal basic characteristics of socialism can and has led to moving away from socialism in a social-democratic direction or in an ultra-left and anarchist direction as during the later years of Mao's leadership.

- **Necessity and chance (or accident).** All objects, processes and phenomena express aspects of both necessity and chance. Necessity expresses itself only through chance or accidental occurrences. The laws of political economy and of historical materialism never occur in pure form, only in and through chance occurrences. Thus the law of value is realized only through the variations of supply and demand. The class struggle expresses an inner necessity of capitalism but every concrete occurrence has its own particularities and is a chance occurrence as it relates to the necessity for the class struggle. Many factors go into each particular expression of class struggle. Their exact coming together to produce the particular acts of class struggle is accidental in relation to the necessity inherent in capitalism that produces one or another form of class struggle at one or another particular time. The basic contradiction of capitalism is that the forces of production (labor power, materials, machines and technology, factories, energy) become more and more interdependent and social while the relations of production (capitalist ownership) are increasingly private, in the hands of a smaller and smaller number of people. One of the results is an anarchistic character of the capitalist reproductive process as a whole. The basic contradiction and anarchistic character of the economic system are necessities that must express themselves, but they do so in an accidental way as to time and form.

To deny necessity is to deny Marxism, to deny there is an objective reality which develops according to necessary laws. Then reality is understood as totally a matter of accident, of great personalities or something similar. If there are no laws of social development, there are none for us to know. We are in a completely voluntarist, rather than law-governed, reality. If, on the other hand, we interpret necessity as a rigid inevitability as to time of happening, form and outcome of struggles in the short run, then we have a rigid, determinist concept of inevitability that does not recognize that necessity takes place only through accidental combinations of circumstances.

This law assumes that conscious activity will sooner or later reflect objective reality, since being is primary and consciousness secondary. Thus sooner or later there will be conscious struggle reflecting real interests. Knowing what is necessity and what is chance is very important to avoid either kind of mistake—assuming that there is no necessity, no laws of social development, no inevitability in social development or that any particular expression of necessity does not involve chance and a particular level of development of consciousness. Every law of social development, every necessity, has as its first assumption that there is social development and it has not been destroyed by nuclear weapons, destruction of the climate or other catastrophes.

- **Cause and effect.** Every object, process or phenomenon has a cause or causes and an effect or effects. Every effect has one or more causes and every cause assumes one or more effects, if it is to be a cause. An effect may also be a cause and every cause may also be an effect and there may be more than one of each. We may not yet know the particular cause or effect. Everything that is chance or accidental in how necessity expresses itself still has particular causes and particular effects. To study a particular event, an effect, we will want to know its immediate causes. But we will also want to know how it expresses some longer-term necessity and why that expression will be accidental in relation to that necessity.

- **Form and content.** Everything has both form and content. Content is closely related to essence—inner character and role in social development. Its outer expression, its cover, the way its essence is held together, is its form. In other words form expresses content. However, form is supposed to fit content, enhance content, correspond to content. Form is not the determining element, but is determined by content. To treat the form as the determining element and compel the content to fit the form, correspond to the form, is formalism. It is not a constant, consistent fit. Sooner or later the two are in contradiction and the content will require a new form that corresponds more easily to its content. Some older content, still applicable, needs new forms that fit new culture to better convey the still necessary content. Thus there is a need to update continually the forms of expression of the necessary content, but one must be sure the new form does in fact fit that content. Nor should form be allowed to diminish content, or substitute a new content for the content still needed. Form does not determine such new content when it is not sound for that reality. This requires a sober estimate whether the same content is still needed and whether the new form helps convey that content, or is in conflict with it and actually is substituting another content. To check this, it is necessary to review whether the existing content is still necessary. Then, do the new forms better convey that content or do they substitute an undesired content? Or are they just new forms for the sake of new forms without enhancing the needed content? Of course such examination may also lead to the conclusion that the old content needs to be replaced or modified to meet new circumstances.

Theory as methodology

In addition to the three main laws of dialectics and the lesser laws or categories, some of which have been discussed, other aspects of Marxism are useful as methodology in working out practical problems of activity. These include the laws and theories of political economy and historical materialism, and the theory of strategy and tactics.

Political economy as methodology. If you know the law of motion of capitalism, the seeking of maximum surplus value to maximize profit, such knowledge will help you figure out the newest methods of the capitalists to squeeze the maximum out of the working class for less. It can help you understand what is coming next in the class struggle.

Historical materialism as methodology. If you know the basic contradiction of capitalism, you will be able to look in advance as to what will be big new problems of capitalism that will affect the lives and struggles of the working class. Knowing the relationship of the base to the superstructure, and the special role played in the super-structure by the state, will help you understand new developments in the state and political structure so you can plan what to do about it.

The theory of strategy and tactics as methodology. Knowing what is a sound strategy for each strategic stage from here to social-ism and knowing the role and principles of tactics can help you answer properly what tactics to pursue to bring the widest masses of the core forces into strategic position with the sound alliances necessary for strategic victories.

Key link in the chain. Lenin said on more than one occasion that political tasks are like a chain. They are all linked together. But it is necessary to pick the correct link at a particular time and grasp it with all your might so that you can pass from one link to the next and move the whole chain. That applies to the national strategy of Marxists, knowing where you are in the succession of necessary and possible strategic stages and concentrating all your effort there, so that with the defeat of the ultra-right, it becomes possible to move on to the next link in the chain, the anti-monopoly struggle, which then opens up the possibility to move on to the final link, the direct struggle for working people's power led by the working class to build socialism.

But the concept of the key link in a chain also applies in assessing where to concentrate effort in a given shop or neighborhood.

Sometimes it is difficult to determine the key link. Several tasks compete as to which is most crucial. Some would list the tasks in a lin-ear order of priority, one through five or six. But life is dialectically interwoven. To determine the key link it is sometimes useful to com-pare each of the main possibilities. What happens to the other very important tasks if you make the first on the list the key link, and what is the impact on the important possible choices? Do that with each possible key link. Usually that helps us understand what is the actual relationship of the links and what should be chosen as the key link for concentration of effort.

Using some or all of the above methodological leads or combina-tions of them, should make it easier and more certain to draw the conclusions necessary to advance the struggle for the interests of the working class and all democratic forces, no matter what the starting situation. The question remains what entity will use the tools of Marxist methodology to put possibilities into action and organize the struggles. This requires social organizations and special ones at that.

7 Organizations Necessary for Winning Progress and Socialism

❖ Organizations for the class and democratic struggles
❖ Trade unions
❖ The Communist Party
❖ The Young Communist League

Organizations for the class and democratic struggles

To win progress and socialism requires many kinds of organizations through which the class and democratic struggle is conducted. Some of these will be temporary organizations for a single action or for a single issue during a particular period. Organizations such as the NAACP, founded in 1909, have played a major role over many years in the struggle of the African American people and other nationally oppressed peoples for freedom and equality, and against racism. Other more short-lived organizations have dealt with aspects of the same struggle. Some women's equality organizations and peace organizations also have a long history. In the last 50 years, a large number of environmental protection organizations have developed and give evidence that they will continue activity as long as there is a severe threat to the environment.

Many working-class community organizations are concerned with struggles over housing, education, health care, utilities, taxes and similar issues. Some last longer than others. Some are strictly local, while some have regional or even national ties. But trade unions are in a special category among the organizations necessary for the struggle for progress.

Trade unions

From the earliest years of trade unions, Marx, Engels and later Lenin recognized them as the primary organizations of the working class, necessary for the daily conduct of the class struggle. Without unions, the worker was alone selling his or her labor power to the capitalist. The power of the capitalist was clearly much greater than that of the individual worker. Not only was the hiring process completely unfair, but the lone worker's ability to enforce the promised wages and benefits and to improve conditions was totally inequitable.

Only when workers combined their collective strength in unions could they begin to win wages, conditions and benefits through collective agreements paying them the value of their labor power as a wage or other specified means of payment. But for this to happen the union had to win recognition and the employer had to bargain with the union to produce the collective bargaining agreement. The struggle continues, including in the legislative arena, to compel the capitalist employer to recognize the union and "bargain in good faith" over a contract. The employer must then be pressed to fulfill the terms of the contract and not undermine it in the relentless quest to maximize profits. So long as capitalism exists, the struggle will continue with the capitalists over organization, bargaining, wages, conditions, benefits and related issues.

Unions also engage in struggle on most other issues of concern to workers. At times unions fight for peace and equality and against racism and sexism, for democratic rights and on many social welfare issues like health care and pensions in the legislative arena and through active participation in elections. Trade unions are and will remain the biggest, most important mass organization of the working class. A major organizing struggle is to enlarge the absolute number and the proportion of workers organized in unions in the U.S. and all capitalist and developing countries. Early in the life of trade unions the issue is often whether trade union consciousness will prevail over tendencies toward class collaboration. Then as socialists and communists come to play a bigger role in the trade unions, fully class-conscious trade unionism will develop out of trade union consciousness. As the organized sector of the working class, labor unions will have to play a leading role in developing the strategic alliances necessary at each stage of social struggle. That role is necessary in the effort to defeat the ultra-right, then in the struggle to radically curb the power of the transnational monopolies as a whole, and then in the struggle for working people's power led by the working class to construct socialism.

The Communist Party

In 1902-03, Lenin put forward the theory of the party of the new type, of the Communist Party, in "What is to be Done" (1902) and other works. In doing so, he drew on the experience of the world Marxist movement that Marx and Engels began in the 1840s and announced in "The Communist Manifesto" (1848), and which continued in the formation of the First International of 1864, the Second International of 1889 and the mass social democratic parties of Europe and the activity of the Russian revolutionary movement. Lenin drew on the proposition from the "Manifesto" that the communists differed from the workers and democratic forces as a whole only because in the struggles for immediate interests they also represent and take care of the future of that movement.

Lenin argued that there was a spontaneous class struggle and that it could and did give birth to trade union consciousness and the trade union movement. Workers learned the need for unions and for trade union unity to protect their daily interests that arose at the point of production. But those spontaneous daily struggles could not give rise to full class consciousness, to socialist consciousness and Marxist ideology in themselves. For that to take place in the working class as a whole so that it could play its historically necessary and possible role, the working-class movement and developments in science, especially social sciences (Marxism), needed to be brought together in a new kind of party, a Communist Party. With the Communist Party developing into the leading force within the working class it would be possible for the working class to lead the way to replace capitalism with socialism, for the working class as a whole to develop full class consciousness, socialist consciousness.

What qualities would the Communist Party need to be able to play such a role? Lenin laid out the basics and they have been further developed since by the world Communist movement. The necessary qualities are:

• The Communist Party is the party of the working class. It acts from the standpoint of the interests of the working class as a whole over the long run. It is rooted in the working class in the first place with a mass base there. It is a part of the working class but also its most advanced section. It is a party of action, of struggle for those interests. It acts in a way so as to unite the maximum of the class and of its allies. It acts in a united front style and builds coalitions. Because it is the party of the working class it is also the party of its most oppressed sections and of its core allies. Therefore, it is also the party of the nationally and racially oppressed, of the women and of the youth, also acting consistently in their interests. The development by the party of a leading role among the working class as a whole is not a matter of self-proclamation or self-seeking. It can exist only as a result of contributions over time that are recognized and welcomed and only for so long as those contributions continue.

• It is the party of socialism. That is its ultimate goal and that goal guides its strategy and tactics.

• Marxism (Leninism), the ideology of the working class, is the ideology of the party. Marxism is the party's guide to action. Marxism consists of the science contained in its philosophy: dialectical and historical materialism, its political economy of capitalism, and in part of the theory of socialist revolution. The final aspect of Marxism is its theory of socialist revolution which includes the policy guides of the party's activity contained in the theory and application of strategy and tactics, and the theory of the party.

• Proletarian internationalism. This means the party opposes all actions of imperialist aggression—political, economic, ideological or military—toward any other people. It sides with the working class and its allies among other peoples and against its own, U.S., imperialism. It is also a partisan of the working class in power in other countries. Within the U.S., proletarian internationalism stands for unity of all nationalities against the capitalists and especially against all forms of special oppression and racist and national chauvinist ideology supporting such oppression and fostering division among the working class and all working people. It supports "workers of the world unite" and "workers and nationally oppressed of the world unite!" (Lenin, 1922).

• Democratic centralism. This is the principle of organization of the Communist Party. Its democratic forms and practices are based on centralism and its centralist forms and practices are based on democracy. Democratic centralism is essential so that the party can arrive at policies that are sound, based on science and on the experience and thinking of the membership and all levels of elected leadership. Its aim is also to realize an organization that is united in action and is a strong, effective force in the class and democratic struggles for whatever is decided. The unity of the party is based on a common agreement about the party's basic nature and direction—unity of will. "Acceptance of the party program" is the basis for membership. This does not mean agreement with everything, mastery of Marxism, or understanding of the whole party program, but rather a willingness to "accept" it.

The convention is the party's highest political body. Its decisions on policy, organization, election of standing leadership, revisions of the basic party program and party constitution are binding on all elected leaders and members. Delegates to the convention are elected from the party's lower organs. The National Committee and officers elected at the National Convention lead the party between conventions in accordance with the decisions of the National Convention. The National Committee elects a National Board as its standing committee to act between plenary meetings of the National Committee within the framework of the National Convention and National Committee decisions. A parallel structure and procedure is followed at the district and lower levels. While all members may hold their own personal opinion on all questions, those elected to leading positions and bodies are elected with the understanding they are to support and carry out the decisions of higher bodies whether or not they personally agree with them.

The exact forms and procedures that embody the principles of democratic centralism are changed from time to time according to circumstances in the given Communist Party. At times when the party was under more severe attack, not only leaders but all members were required to carry out decisions whether they agreed with them or not. At other times, members were bound not to act or campaign against decisions already taken, but they were not bound to carry out all decisions. Factionalism, however, is not permitted in a Communist Party at any time. A faction is a group of people who are organized to change party policy, leadership or activity by violating or by-passing party procedures and organization.

The forms of democratic membership input before decisions vary according to circumstance. During the pre-convention discussion period, all past policies, practices and actions of leading bodies and individuals are subject to review and may be questioned, as well as new proposals and policies put forward.

Democratic centralism is connected with collectivity as a style of work in reaching policy decisions and carrying out work. Collectivity is the opposite of one-person decision-making on substantial questions. Collectivity, however, also requires individual leadership responsibility so that the collective will finds expression and is carried out. Collectivity in policy-making guards against the one-sidedness of individual experience and viewpoint. It is a necessary condition for a sound, rounded Marxist viewpoint. Collectivity in carrying out policy decisions helps assure success through maximum participation in activity and helps prevent one-sidedness and subjectivity in work. Collectivity in evaluating work and policies is also important to assure that the collectively determined policies have been put to the test of practice and conclusions drawn collectively.

Criticism and self-criticism is also closely connected with democratic centralism. Regular review and evaluation of all major policies, decisions and work are a major part of the style of work of the Communist Party, to learn from experience, avoid big mistakes and not repeat significant mistakes. Where possible, the individual responsible to lead particular work should evaluate it—what was successful and done well and what were the weaknesses and mistakes. A collective evaluation allows others to participate in the process, helping everyone to learn what was done well, and what needs improvement or correction for the future.

Democratic centralism takes different forms in other organizations of working-class struggle. Thus a union requires all members to support a strike whether or not they personally agree it is a good idea. Strikebreakers are not allowed. The point is to have strong democratic input and control, but also a strong ability to act in unity in tough class battles.

The concept of concentration is closely related to democratic centralsim and the principles of organization of the Communist Party. There are different kinds of concentration with different aims. They all imply the mustering of resources, human and material, and a style of work for everyone in order to accomplish certain objectives. There is concentration of effort in struggles around particular issues or demands in relation to jobs, equality, democracy, peace, etc. There can also be concentration of effort to fulfill a fund drive or other task connected with building the Communist Party.

Industrial concentration is perhaps the best known form. Its aim is to build particular clubs, membership and influence of the Communist Party among the most decisive sections of the working class. Over time, the role that certain industries play in the economy changes, as do local economic factors, and the practical ability of the Party nationally and locally to carry out a concentration policy.

Concentration means not only special attention to and help for the Party members already workers in the selected shop or industry, but trying to bring additional human and material resources to bear on the problem, and to reach workers in the communities where they live. Such an effort can involve one or more clubs, a district, the whole national Party, or some combination ot these forces.

The Communist Party has also pursued a policy of triple concentration in relation to the most decisive communities of the nationally and racially oppressed. Resources from the national Party, district and clubs are applied to develop clubs in these selected areas.

In the course ot concentration work, the mass strategic and tactical policies as applied in the labor movement or oppressed communities are pursued. The aim remains to build particular Communist Party clubs. For most members, their activity takes place where they live and/or work, where it is most natural for them to be active. At the same time, they look for ways to help the concentration efforts, as well as make more direct contributions to concentration work.

How has Lenin's theory of the party of the new type fared in practice? In most countries the Communist Parties made and still make substantial contributions to the working class and democratic forces in their struggles for daily living needs, for peace, democracy, equality of the nationally oppressed and other issues. In our country, the Communist Party played a major role in organizing the mass production industries and many other unions and in all the great strike struggles. It was also a factor in the New Deal legislation that helped the small farmers and an important force in winning Social Security and other New Deal welfare legislation as well as the Wagner Act to protect labor's rights. It played an outstanding role in fighting lynchings and other racist violence and Jim Crow practices. Its internationalism was outstanding in the fight for peace and against fascism. This included the effort to break the anti-Soviet Cordon Sanitaire alliance and win diplomatic and economic relations with the first working-class state, the USSR. It acted to oppose Italian fascist aggression in Ethiopia and together with the YCL led the fight in solidarity with Republican Spain, playing a big role in the Lincoln Brigade volunteers. Many party and YCL members fought in Spain and in World War II. The party fought valiantly against the Cold War and McCarthyism. It pioneered in the fight for women's rights.

In 1946-48 the Communist Party reached its peak membership of close to 100,000 and had considerable strength in labor and all-people's movements. But as a result of McCarthyism and the Cold War and anti-communist climate, the party steadily lost many members. But it was not only the party and organizations closely associated with it that were damaged or driven out of existence during McCarthyism and the Cold War. There was hardly an area of U.S. democratic life that was not seriously harmed by the witch-hunt. The CIO was split and several important unions were gradually destroyed. The impact on Hollywood and the whole entertainment industry is especially well-known.

Over 200 Communist Party leaders were indicted and many spent years in prison or as fugitives. Many others went to jail for contempt of Congress or other "crimes" derivative of the witch-hunt. Large numbers were deported as "undesirable aliens." Thousands lost their jobs, underwent family harassment and had difficulty earning a living. Ethel and Julius Rosenberg were executed during the witch-hunt. It has been revealed that the government knew Ethel Rosenberg did not commit any crime. What Julius Rosenberg apparently did in 1944 was known to the government for years. He apparently was not prosecuted, because it related to a then war-time ally and had nothing to do with the secret of the atomic bomb.

As a result of the 1956-57 revelations about the Stalin regime and related internal strife, the party suffered further losses. But even with the loss of members, the party continued to be active not only against the "red scare" repression but also in the struggle for peace, and made a contribution much beyond its numbers to prevent nuclear war with the Soviet Union, to end the Korean War, to end the Vietnam War, to end the interventions against Cuba, and, much later, to the struggle to end the aggression against Iraq and Afghanistan.

The Communist Party was a factor in the development of the "fresh winds" in labor that replaced the George Meany-type of class-collaboration union leadership with the forward-looking John Sweeney leadership. The CPUSA supported the workers in strike struggles and fought for the needs of the unemployed especially during recessions. Struggles for health care, education, affordable housing and other working class community needs always found Communist Party support.

The party fought for school desegregation and to implement the Supreme Court decision of Brown v. Board of Education and for the civil rights legislation guaranteeing the right to vote, and other laws. It supported and participated in the Civil Rights revolution in the South and for the rights of undocumented immigrant workers. Communists led the presentation of the "We Charge Genocide" petition to the United Nations in 1950. The party was also active in the main struggles for women's equality, including reproductive rights, equal pay for equal work and work of comparable value, and day care.

The CPUSA fought for, and with others won the freedom of Angela Davis. Angela Davis was a young Black activist, academic and member of the Communist Party. She was falsely indicted for murder in connection with a death in a prison break, a prosecution also connected with the persecution of the Black Panther Party. When the ultra-right political trend developed, took control of the Republican Party and won the 1980 national elections, the party called for and fought to build an all-people's front of center, progressive and left forces to defeat it and expel it from government. George W. Bush's victory in 2000 meant even stronger ultra-right control over the whole government and attacks on all previous gains. Soon after, the Al Qaeda attack on Sept. 11, 2001 became a new excuse for neoconservative international and domestic policy, U.S. imperialism attacked Afghanistan and then Iraq. The Communist Party continued to be the most consistent fighter on the left for the broadest unity to defeat the ultra-right. With labor in the lead and with the African American and Latino peoples, women and youth, the 2006 Congressional elections defeated the ultra-right hold on Congress and set the stage to exclude this trend from control of the Executive Branch in the 2008 elections. As noted in Chapter 5, the Communist Party was active in the 2008 election defeat of the ultra-right.

Did the Communist Parties make mistakes? Of course, all of them did as did all other democratic, progressive, left and socialist forces.

There are the daily errors of tactics that creep in mainly from lack of concrete knowledge of the situation. There were also errors of immaturity in the first years of the communist parties, when they knew little of the foundations of Marxism laid by Marx, Engels and Lenin. In the U.S. at first the concept was to win the working class alone to fight the capitalist class. It took a while to learn from our own experience and study, as well as from Lenin and the Soviet experience, that the working class had potential allies in the farmers (family farmers, share-croppers and tenant farmers) and the nationally oppressed starting with the African American people. Then the CPUSA made an original theoretical and strategic contribution to the world communist movement, as discussed in Chapter 5, that the monopoly section of the capitalists had become fully dominant in the economic, political and ideological sphere. It should be singled out as the enemy in the developed capitalist countries and a coalition built of all the non-monopoly forces to radically curb its power and open up the path to socialism. This concept was updated and developed further in 1980 and again in the 2000 elections and after, with the all-people's front against the ultra-right. (See Chapter 5.)

Most of the world Communist movement including the CPUSA did not think independently enough and followed too closely the theoretical and sometimes the practical lead of the Soviet Union. A certain tendency to "copy" was understandable and natural. After all the Soviet Union was the first workers' state and break in world capitalism. The USSR was surrounded by world capitalism, threatened and then viciously attacked by Nazi Germany and its allies, and then faced down nuclear war and Churchill and Truman's Cold War. The USSR made huge improvements in the everyday lives of its people— education, health care, better housing and jobs—which put pressure on the capitalist countries to raise workers' living standards. But everything it did and did not do was slandered. No wonder we did not believe most of the slanders. No wonder we and all of progressive humanity, Communist and not, looked to the Soviet Union for leadership and help in the fight for peace and progress.

But we did not think independently enough and did not ask enough questions. The Khrushchev report on the Stalin group came as a shock, and we did not thoroughly examine and digest all that flowed from these revelations, especially about the growing problems of the

Soviet model of a socialist economy and the political structures that went with it. As a result we were again surprised by the differences among the Soviet Communists, and then at the collapse of the Soviet Union and other Eastern European socialist countries. The Communist Parties have learned from that defeat and there is no longer considered to be any leading party or country of socialism. Most of the Stalinist distortions of theory and policy have been cleaned out by most of the world Communist movement including the CPUSA.

The CPUSA for a period of time took wrong positions on some issues but then made corrections. These included the position discussed in Chapter 4 over the Nazi-Soviet Pact of 1939, the failure to protest the internment of Japanese residents in concentration camps during World War II, and the failure for a number of years to fully defend the rights of the LGBT community.

How has Lenin's proposition fared that the spontaneous working-class struggle cannot come to full class consciousness and win socialism without the leading role of a Communist Party, the kind of party Lenin outlined? As with all theoretical conclusions and laws, with time they appear in considerably different form than originally expected, and never in the pure form that theory originally projects. And for some time a rigid Stalin-type reading of Lenin's idea was current in the world Communist movement. Others, not only the Communist Party, may play a role in developing such socialist class consciousness. That might be a left-wing socialist party as in the German Democratic Republic and several other Eastern European countries. In Cuba the 26th of July Movement, which included a Marxist current, played that role both before and after the victory of power, alongside the Popular Socialist Party (the first Communist Party of Cuba). The process of unification of the July 26th Movement and the PSP on a Marxist basis to form the second Communist Party went through several stages before it was completed in 1975. That is another variation of Lenin's theory of the existence of a law requiring the unique role of a Communist Party. It operated, but life's complications and accidents brought it to operate differently over a considerable period of time.

It appears the process will be fundamentally the same in a number of Latin American countries, but with even wider variations in how it will take place and how long it will take to accomplish. We can expect the process will have its own unique features in the U.S. It is likely there will be one or more other socialist parties playing a positive role in alliance with the CPUSA and that may well last for a long time before the parties achieve unity on the basis of Marxism. How that might happen is likely to be quite different from anywhere else in the world. But it will remain basically true that the working class as a whole cannot come to socialist consciousness based only on its own spontaneous daily struggle but will require existing among its ranks a mass communist party of socialism that will supply the scientific tools, experience and organization to combine with the working-class movement and result in socialist consciousness and what is needed to keep advancing in the face of many challenges and difficulties. The Communist Party will certainly play a necessary role in the consistent pursuit of the interests of the working class, of all working people and of humanity.

There are no complete exceptions to Lenin's rule about the need for a Communist Party to win and construct socialism. Even the biggest variations on the rule will only prove the rule, that necessity is at work in whatever variations occur. The leading role of a Communist Party is not something achieved and maintained by self-proclamation. It has to be won in practice and continually reestablished in the life of class and democratic struggles.

Thus we have to say that capitalism and its horrors will remain until a mass Communist Party is built that can play a key role in producing socialist class consciousness and do what is needed to achieve working people's power led by the working class. As discussed earlier, it is also likely that non-socialist parties will exist in the transition to socialism and perhaps long into its construction.

The Young Communist League

Lenin posed the question whether it was possible to win the young generation to socialism by the activity of the Communist Party alone. He concluded it was not possible because "necessarily the youth must come to socialism in different ways, by other paths, in other forms, under other circumstances than their fathers [and mothers—DR]. Incidentally, this is why we must be decidedly in favor of the organizational independence of the youth league."

Lenin called for the "organizational independence," but not the political and ideological independence of the youth league. The party was to lead the fight for the interests of the working class and all its allies, for young workers as well as older ones and for the young generation as a whole. Partly this is to be done by winning labor and all its allies to support youth's needs and thereby to win them to labor's side. This requires supporting youth in its fight for its special needs so that youth have a real future. The party also leads the fight for the youth as it does for all age groups, through its leading members who are also elected leaders of the YCL. It helps lead it through developing the national strategic policy at all stages of the struggle and its role in developing Marxist ideology for all generations and sectors of the working people, including the youth.

The youth are not in a position to develop independently their own strategic policy for the whole country, for the whole working class and working people. They are not in a position to develop Marxist ideology as a whole. Undoubtedly they will contribute to their application and further development as they apply to youth. They are not in a position to do more than this as they represent only one age segment of the working class and are a multi-class organization by nature. The nature of the YCL is that it is in the process of learning Marxism and socialism, open to people who are just exploring the subject and to people who join because of its action on a single issue or its provision of cultural and sports activities. That is different from the nature of the Communist Party. Its role and character are more limited. It is not in a position and does not try to work out strategic policy for the whole movement or policy on issues that do not involve youth in a special way. Those joining the YCL do not master or even accept Marxism necessarily by joining the YCL. They agree only to be open to it.

But the YCL has a major role to play in uniting the young generation internally, with young workers playing the leading role. It has a major role in uniting the young generation with the working class and labor movement and with the nationally oppressed and women, with labor in the lead, to be part of the core forces to win working people as a whole for each stage of strategy and struggle from here to socialism. Thus the building of a mass YCL becomes critical both for the future growth of the movement and for the struggle for socialism and, for the future growth of the Communist Party and for the winning of the young generation to the side of the working class in the struggle for progress and socialism.

The Communist Party tries to do everything it can to help the YCL grow and develop. It should do this through a mutual championing and through comradely political and ideological guidance in a non-know-it-all way. The YCL elected leadership will know how concretely to apply the general to the youth and through what forms and culture.

Engels said:

"Is it not natural that youth should predominate in our party, the revolutionary party? We are the party of the future and the future belongs to the youth. We are the party of the innovators, and it is always the youth who most eagerly follow the innovators. We are a party that is waging a self-sacrificing struggle against what is old and decaying, and youth is always the first to undertake a self-sacrificing struggle." (Engels, quoted in Lenin, "The Crisis of Menshevism," 1906, CW, Vol. 11, p. 354)

Glossary

All people's front against the ultra right – this is the strategy developed by the Communist Party USA against the most reactionary sector of the transnational monopolies represented by the Bush administration. The strategy consisted of uniting the core forces of the working class, the nationally oppressed, women, youth and all other sections of working people and even the more moderate section of the transnationals to defeat the ultra right.

Anti-monopoly coalition – in the second stage of the CPUSA's strategy, the aim is to radically curb the power of the transnational monopolies as a whole. To do that an even wider coalition of the core forces led by labor and the working class and supported by all non-monopoly sectors of the population will be required along with a people's party led by labor and not including any section of monopoly. This second stage would then lead to the third stage, the struggle for working people's power led by the working class in order to construct socialism.

Balance of forces – at the level of the country as a whole, and with respect to all issues and struggles, it refers to an estimate of all the class and social forces who are on the side of progress as compared to those who are on the side of a retrograde direction for the country and those who may be not committed in either direction. The balance may be considered on a given national issue or in relation to a local struggle. In this case, the balance is not only in terms of class and social forces, but must take into account particular political tendencies and particular movements and organizations.

Basis, or base – the entirety of the production relations, or class relations of a specific socioeconomic formation, constitutes the basis of that formation. On the basis of each formation a superstructure develops, the dominant ideas and institutions of which support and defend the interests of the class that is dominant in the basis. See Superstructure.

Classes – "Large groups of people differing from each other by the place they occupy in the historically determined system of social production, by their relations (in most cases fixed and formulated in law) to the means of production, by their role in the social organization of labor, and consequently, by the dimensions of the share of social wealth of which they dispose and the mode of acquiring it." V.I. Lenin, A Great Beginning, July 1913, CW Vol. 29, p. 421.

Class struggle – is waged between classes whose interests are incompatible or contradictory; is the basic content of and the driving force behind the development of all antagonistic class societies. It is waged in the political, economic and ideological spheres in a multitude of forms.

Commodity – is a material or immaterial object produced for exchange either for another object or for a money equivalent. It has both use and exchange value. See the law of value below.

Core forces – The Communist Party USA applies this term to the most important class and social forces for social progress. These include the working class, the nationally and racially oppressed, women and youth.

Democracy – Originally democracy meant the political rule of the people no matter what its form or details. It has also come to apply not only to the political aspects of society but also to the economic, cultural and ideological aspects. It has become clear that the type of socioeconomic formation greatly influenced every aspect of democracy, whether ancient slave society, feudal, capitalist or socialist. Democracy existed for the ruling class of each socioeconomic formation but was not existent for the economically exploited and oppressed classes or was quite limited by the property relations and resulting political-state structure.

Yet democracy for working people under capitalist ownership and domination of the political process was of great importance to the working class, giving it room to struggle for its daily needs and for more fundamental change. Fascism did not permit such activity but rather suppressed it. Other authoritarian regimes under "bourgeois democracy" permitted the exercise of some democratic rights but limited them. In modern society, democracy has become a prime need of working people on the order of all other necessities of life. Socialism, with social ownership of the means of production, provides the potential for a vast expansion of political, economic and social democracy in all spheres of life.

Dialectical materialism – See materialism. It is the philosophy of Marxism; it is a materialism that shows how and why social life, nature and thought develop and undergo both quantitative and qualitative changes. It also constitutes the heart of the methodology of Marxism. It provides universal laws of change and development.

Dictatorship of the proletariat – is the phrase used by Marx, Engels and Lenin to describe the kind of state power that would follow capitalism in the construction of socialism and would exist until there were no longer internal or external threats by contending classes to the development of communist society, a society without contending classes or any state proper. The Communist Party USA and many other communist parties no longer use this phrase and substitute for it phrases like "working people's power led by the working class." Construction of socialism requires leadership of the state power apparatus by the working class together with its allies. In the U.S. that would include the nationally and racially oppressed, women, youth and others. It would be a state infinitely more democratic than any under capitalism. The function of such a state would be to enforce the constitution and laws so that the representatives of the old system, capitalism, could not violate those rules to restore the old system through a coup d'etat or similar means.

Doctrinairism – is a departure from Marxism in which theoretical and political conclusions sound for prior situations are mechanically applied to new developments for which they are not appropriate. Doctrinairism usually moves in a leftist direction but it can also be used to uphold rightist positions.

Dogmatism – represents rigidity in method, in politics and/or in practice. It refuses to respond to change and development. It usually moves in a leftist direction but can also go in a right direction, depending on what it is that is treated in a dogmatic manner and what the actual circumstances are.

Driving forces of historical development – the social forces (popular masses, classes, parties) capable of carrying out tasks posed by history, including the reasons impelling these forces to act, such as, first and foremost, social requirements, interests, goals and ideas.

Economic crisis – under capitalism periodic economic crises take place. These involve the capitalists overproducing during the boom period relative to effective demand in their attempt to achieve maximum profits by securing a greater proportion of the market under the conditions of anarchy, without definite knowledge of what other capitalist producers are doing. The crisis point is reached when the capitalists realize there is a substantial imbalance between production and effective demand and they all begin to reduce production to put it in line with demand. Those actions themselves then feed a further reduction in effective demand and a vicious circle. Finally, production is put in rough balance with demand at a very low level of the economy. Attempts to reduce costs of production with new machinery and technology, along with increasing wages and spending for those producing the new technology, then create the possibility of rising demand and production, until the cycle is repeated. No two cycles are alike in detail.

Economic determinism – the philosophical view that economic developments alone determine all other developments in society and do so directly, without any mediating influences. Marxism was accused of being "economic determinist" but Marx and Engels often explained their opposition to such a view. They illustrated, in concretely examining particular historical developments, that they always took into account the influence of all kinds of factors, political, cultural, national, ideological, personal, etc. Still, they asserted that in the sweep of development of society, underlying laws exist about the mode of production of the necessities of life that have the greatest (but not sole) long-term influence.

Ethics – a philosophical discipline dealing with morality. In societies with contending classes, ethical principles are closely related to the interests of these classes.

Exploitation – appropriation by some of the products of labor of others, the immediate producers; it is inherent in all antagonistic societies. In capitalist society the capitalist owners of the means of production are able to exploit the workers who create the material or immaterial commodities because they own the means of production and hire workers who are to be paid less than the value of what they produce, the excess being the property of the capitalist owners. The unpaid labor of the workers in the sphere of circulation of commodities enables the capitalist to realize some surplus value created by the workers in the sphere of production of commodities. In that sense these workers are also exploited, though they do not produce commodities.

Fascism – is one of the two basic forms of capitalist state and political rule; the other being "bourgeois democracy." It is a form of state rule in which there is open terrorist rule by the most reactionary, militarist, chauvinist section of big capital.

Financialization – is a new qualitative development of state monopoly capitalism closely associated with the development of its "globalization" or "transnationalization" phase. The financial sector of capitalism—banks, investment firms, hedge funds and others—becomes the economically dominant form of extracting profit from the unpaid labor of workers and from all other working people and all other sectors of monopoly capital. It involves a high level of speculation and parasitism and instability. It exercises a great deal of influence over the government and seeks to remove all controls and open the path for all kinds of financial instruments based on such speculation, securitization of property mortgages, derivatives, credit default swaps, etc. It separates itself from concern for the financing of the production of material commodities.

Freedom, social – human activity based on knowledge of the operation of objective laws of social development. Engels liked to say, "Freedom is the recognition of necessity."

Fundamental question of philosophy – the relation of thinking to being, consciousness to matter, the ideal to the material. Materialists hold that being is primary and consciousness is secondary or reflective of being.

Globalization (transnationalization) – On the basis of development of new technology, transportation and materials, capitalism in the 1970s came to be dominated by a few hundred transnational monopolies based in the U.S. and the other major capitalist powers. These transnational industrial, banking and merchandizing corporations functioned in many countries at the same time, often dominating the same type of economic activity in each. They could cut production very rapidly in some countries while increasing it in others.

A whole system of international economic and political measures to facilitate the profit-seeking activities of the transnationals grew up producing an overall "globalization" of the world economic and political structure. The spread of neoliberalism was associated with globalization. Neoliberalism meant privatization of many formerly government activities into the hands of the transnationals.

Idealism – the general name for philosophical doctrines maintaining that spirit, consciousness, mental activity are primary, while matter, nature, physical activity are secondary and derivative.

Ideology – a system of political, legal, moral, philosophical, religious and artistic ideas and views, which has a pronounced class character. In antagonistic formations, the dominating ideology of the exploiter classes is posed against the ideology of the exploited classes. The ideologists of the exploiting classes try to conceal the class character of their ideology and to represent it as supra-class and non-party. Marxism maintains no classless ideology can exist in a class-divided society. Ideology reflects social relations between people and actively influences the evolution of social life.

Imperialism – at the end of the 19th and beginning of the 20th centuries "free" competitive capitalism developed into monopoly capitalism, which Lenin termed "imperialism, the highest and last stage of capitalism." He found imperialism had five characteristics: domination by giant monopoly corporations, merger of banking and industrial capital with banking becoming a dominant finance capital, export of capital as well as of commodities, division of the world economically, division of the world politically by military means and its redivision. Imperialism was not only a policy of the monopoly capitalist powers, it was a stage of development of capitalism. It was the source of wars and world wars.

Interests – a form of expression and awareness of people's needs as manifested in their behavior and activity to satisfy these needs. People are not always as yet aware of their interests. Each class has common interests, as do specially oppressed sections of the population such as the nationally oppressed, women and youth. Personal interests usually fit with class interests but in individual cases can conflict with class interests. False understanding of interests, a mis-understanding of what they really are, is often influenced by the propaganda and ideological activity of class opponents.

Internationalism – international solidarity of workers, working people and communists of all countries in their struggle for common goals, and their solidarity with peoples fighting for their national liberation and social progress, based on strict observance of the principle of equality and independence of each of the peoples. Specific forms of internationalism include anti-imperialist, proletarian, socialist and communist.

Materialism – a philosophical trend maintaining that the world is material and objective, and exists externally and independently of human consciousness, that matter is primary, not created, and is eternal, that consciousness and thinking are a property of matter and that the world and its laws are knowable.

Means of production – is the aggregate of the material elements of the productive forces, as distinct from the living element of production, i.e. the workers. The means of production includes first, the objects of labor, the objects people work on. These are mainly raw materials which have already been changed to some extent by people's labor. Second, it includes the means of labor—the aggregate of material elements people use to influence the objects of labor (work tools, workshops, transport, warehouses for raw materials and finished products, arable land). The most important means of labor are the instruments of labor which indicate the degree of development of the social production forces, and the social relations under which labor takes place. The instruments of production change most rapidly.

Mediation – Mediation occurs in social development when one phenomenon like the economy influences much else, often not directly but through other influences like the political structure. There may be more than one mediating cause or influence and more than one level of mediation.

Mode of production of material benefits – a historically-conditioned manner of producing material benefits, representing specific unity of the production forces and production relations.

Nation – a historically-formed community of people typically formed during the development of capitalism and socialism. It consists of a common economy which is most important in bringing about a common territory, common language, common culture and resulting common traits of national character. According to Leninism, the nation has a right to self-determination, to determine how it will achieve political freedom and equality. This right includes having its own nation-state. The communists of an oppressor nation need to support the right of an oppressed nation to decide how best it will achieve freedom and equality, whether by separation or through various democratic forms within the existing state. The communists of the oppressed people decide whether separation or equality within the old state is preferable from the standpoint of the interests of the working class of both nations.

Nationality – An historically-formed community of people typically formed prior to capitalism. Elements of a common economy exist but this characteristic is unstable. It also has a common territory, common language and common culture. According to Lenin a nationality also has the right to self-determination in one or another form short of a separate nationality-state, which a nationality is incapable of sustaining in a hostile capitalist world and which may encroach on the rights of other nationalities or on those of the nation-state within which it exists.

Nature – in the broadest sense, the sum total of things, the world in the diversity of its manifestations; in a narrower sense, the sum total of biological conditions of the existence of human society.

Necessity, historical – processes and phenomena conditioned by essential features and laws of society, which are expressed through chance or accidental events not directly conditioned by the particular historical necessity.

Objective historical conditions – those conditions of life, society and historical development that are independent of the will of individuals, classes or parties. Material economic conditions—the level and character of the productive forces and corresponding productive relations—are primary and fundamental objective historical conditions.

Opportunism – the theory and practice of reconciliation with the bourgeoisie, of making the workers' movement serve the interests of the bourgeoisie and contribute to the preservation and strengthening of its positions. This is not to be confused with the process of development of consistent class consciousness by the workers as a whole and by their leaders, first to trade-union consciousness, and then to more and more consistent class consciousness, including socialist, Marxist and communist consciousness. Opportunism is a static, hardened outlook that seeks to adjust the struggle of the workers to the interests of the capitalists. Opportunism is usually in a right direction but there are also examples of "left' opportunism.

Philosophy – a form of social consciousness aimed at elaborating a system of ideas, a world outlook and a view of humankind's place in it. It has a class orientation in class society.

Political consciousness – a system of ideas and views, sentiments, aims and tasks manifested in the activity of classes and social groups.

Political Economy - Is the science of the development of socio production, i.e., economic relations between people in the process of production. It clarifies the laws governing production, distribution, exchange and consumption in human society, and various stages of its development, such as the political economy of capitalism.

Politics – activity relating to the sphere of relations between classes, nations and other social groups which comprises winning, retention or use of state power, participation in governing of the state, and working out of the forms, tasks and content of state power.

Popular masses – the workers and other social groups capable of accomplishing progressive change in various spheres of the life of society by virtue of their objective status and interests in society. In the U.S. they include the core forces: the working class, the nationally and racially oppressed, women, youth, and everyone except big capital. Among them are small farmers, small business people, self-employed, seniors, the LGBT community, the disabled and others.

Production relations – the totality of material, economic relations that are formed between people in the process of social production and the delivery of social products from producer to consumer.

Production forces – the totality of subjective (people) and material (means of production) elements reflecting the active relation of man to nature.

Profit – expresses the relationship in production of the surplus value (unpaid work) to the variable capital (wages) and the fixed capital (raw materials, use of energy, plant, etc.) in the production process. Marx calls it a transmuted form of surplus value.

Progress, social – a law-governed, onward movement of society from lower to higher stages and forms of the life of society, from an obsolete to a new economic system. It is progressive rather than simply repetitive because social progress builds on what continues to be useful from past social formations.

Proletariat – originally this term was applied to the great bulk of workers who worked together in large numbers in mass production industries, and who did not own any of the means of production. More recently the term has been replaced by the "working class." It applies to all sectors of the class who do not own the means of production or the means of distribution and whose unpaid labor enables one or another section of the capitalist class to realize a proportion of the surplus value created by the workers in the sphere of production of both material and immaterial commodities. This includes not only those previously considered proletarian but also such categories as teachers, health care workers, scientific and technical nonmanagerial workers.

Reductionism – is a tendency in philosophy, historiography and other fields to reduce all social causation to one cause such as economic, or to the action and interests of the working class and the class struggle alone. This oversimplifies causation in social development and overlooks other immediate or intermediate causes and thereby distorts reality. It "reduces" everything to the single cause.

Revisionism – is a system of political thought and activity, usually in the area of theory, that finds the theoretical propositions of Marxism and Leninism to require basic changes due to alleged changes in reality when such changes have not taken place, so that those propositions of Marxism remain valid. Asserting that the working class is no longer capable of performing the leading role for social progress would be an example of revisionism. Revisionism is usually in an opportunist direction to the right but can also be in a sectarian direction to the left.

Revolutionary process, world – the unfolding process of transition from capitalism to socialism the world over which emerges from the struggle of the working class and its allies in the developed capitalist countries, the struggle of the oppressed peoples for full independence and development, the struggle of the developing countries for development and full equality, and the struggle of the countries building or developing socialism to continually advance. All of this is part of the revolutionary process that objectively moves from capitalism to socialism.

Scientific & technological revolution – radical qualitative change in the productive forces as science becomes a direct productive force.

Sectarianism – pursuit by the progressive and revolutionary forces of strategic and tactical policies and ways of working that unnecessarily isolate them from wider sections of the working class and popular masses. Wrong theory can have the same result. Sectarianism usually expresses itself in a leftist direction, though it can also be in a right direction.

Social being – material interrelations between people and between people and nature that emerge with the development of human society.

Social consciousness – the intellectual plane of historical process; a reflection of social being manifested in different historically-rooted forms. It consists of two levels, social psychology and ideology, and it has many forms—political, legal, philosophical, ethical, aesthetic, religious.

Social laws – objective, recurring and essential links between phenomena of the life of society characterizing the ongoing movement of society.

Social revolution – an objective law of transition from an obsolete to a new and progressive socioeconomic system. A radical change in the system of social relations, it resolves urgent sociopolitical and socioeconomic contradictions. In class society social revolution begins with a change in which class(es) hold state power and concludes with new productive relations becoming predominant.

Socioeconomic formation – a definite stage in the historical development of society; a specific historical type of society such as ancient slave society, feudalism, capitalism, socialism.

Soviet – the Russian word for "council." In the development of the Russian Revolution of Nov. 7, 1917, the workers, the poor peasants, the army and the navy each formed their own councils throughout the country which embodied both policy-making and organizational functioning for action to challenge the interests of czardom and the bourgeois constituent assembly. Some were led by the Bolshevik Party, some by the Menshevik Party and a small number by others. When the Bolsheviks gained the majority, they were able to lead the successful revolution. The state formation of the victorious revolution was that of local, republic and all-union Soviets in which the legislative and executive functions were subordinate to the Soviets representing the class and social forces who won the revolution. Later the two all-union Soviets were called the Soviet of the People and the Soviet of Nationalities.

Special oppression – Capitalism produces not only exploitation and oppression of the entire working class. It adds to this special forms of oppression and extra exploitation (super exploitation) with respect to the nationally and racially oppressed, women, youth and others. The working-class sector of these groups suffers the same exploitation and oppression as the whole working class but also special oppression, inferior wages for comparable work, etc. and the non-working class sectors of the specially oppressed experience special oppression in living conditions, culture, etc.

Spontaneity, historical – processes and phenomena not controlled by the laws of social development, nor by the activity of the conscious Marxist parties and forces.

State – the principal institutions of the political system in class society exercising administration of society and safeguarding the economic and social system; in antagonistic class society the state is run by the class which possesses economic power and employs it to maintain that economic system in the face of its antagonists.

State monopoly capitalism – capitalism in its monopoly capitalist stage comes to merge its economy with the state, creating a qualitatively new phase of monopoly capitalism, state monopoly capitalism. The state becomes a direct participant in helping the monopoly capitalists realize surplus value and profit. At this point in development, the merger can help the system ameliorate the social conditions that weigh heavily on working people, providing unemployment compensation, social security, etc. The state is no longer limited to holding power and suppressing any challenges.

Strategy – determines the balance of social forces and what would constitute a qualitative turn in social development or in the struggle for progress. It then determines what class and social forces will oppose the strategic goal of the progressive forces and which class and social forces can be won to the side of the working class in the struggle for the goal. All of this constitutes the strategy, the strategic policy, line or plan. Tactics are required to bring the necessary social forces together against the main opponent and conduct successful struggle.

Subjective factor of history – totality of phenomena and human activity entirely derived from people's will and consciousness; scientific knowledge of social phenomena and various forms of conscious organization and engagement in the social process. The Communist Party is the leading political organization reflecting the conscious subjective factor.

Subjectivism – approach in cognition or practice ignoring the objective laws of the surrounding world; its core is absolutization of the role of the subject and subjective activity in the life of society; subjectivism in policies is manifested in arbitrariness (the will of the subject as set off against the objective conditions).

Superstructure – a system of ideological relations and views (political, legal, moral, cultural, religious) and corresponding institutions (the state, political parties, etc.) that reflects the basis (also called the base) of the socioeconomic formation. The dominant views and institutions in the superstructure serve and defend the dominant class in the basis of class-divided societies. The rising class and social forces are the source of a challenging superstructure that gradually grows up. Some reverse influence exists of superstructure to basis and from the productive forces through the basis to the superstructure.

Surplus value – what the worker sells the capitalist is his or her ability to labor, not the value of what the worker produces. This labor power is a commodity and as a commodity its value is the average cost of the commodities needed to reproduce that level of labor skill, and meet the needs of the family as part of what it takes to reproduce that labor. The worker is paid the value of the labor power as the wage. The capitalist hires the worker because in the process of production the worker produces a surplus value—the difference between the wage or value of labor power paid and the value of what is produced—which belongs to the capitalist because of ownership of the means of production. This is surplus value, the unpaid labor of the worker.

Tactics – must serve strategy. Tactics deals with the issues and demands that are selected, the forms of struggle and organization picked to bring together the social forces needed for the strategy. Tactics not subordinated to strategy lacks direction.

Theory – is a system of generalized ideas underlying a department of knowledge.

Value, law of – the law of value which Marx took over from David Ricardo and others and further developed asserts that commodities exchange at value or for the money equivalent of the value embodied in a given commodity. The value (or exchange value) of a commodity is measured by the average labor time embodied in the production of the commodity.

War – organized armed struggle between states, (groups of states), classes, or nations (peoples). War is a continuation of class policy by violent means. Now no class can pursue nuclear war and hope to achieve its class policy since nuclear war can destroy all property and human life.